WESTMINSTER AND BEYOND

Westminster and Beyond

Based on the B.B.C. Radio Series 'Talking Politics'

ANTHONY KING
University of Essex

and

ANNE SLOMAN
B.B.C.

First published 1973 by
THE MACMILLAN PRESS LTD
London and Basingstoke
Associated companies in New York Dublin Melbourne Johannesburg and Madras

SBN 333 14492 9

Printed in Great Britain by
WESTERN PRINTING SERVICES LTD
Bristol

TO STEVE BONARJEE

In affection and gratitude

Contents

The Authors

ANTHONY KING has been Professor of Government at the University of Essex since 1969 and is Editor of the *British Journal of Political Science.* He was formerly a Fellow of Magdalen College, Oxford. He edited *The British Prime Minister* (Macmillan, 1970) and is co-author with David Butler of *The British General Election of 1964* (Macmillan, 1965) and *The British General Election of 1966* (Macmillan, 1966). A regular contributor to B.B.C. Radio programmes, he has also written on British politics and elections for the *Observer*, the *Spectator*, and *New Society.*

ANNE SLOMAN was a producer of political programmes on B.B.C. Radio 4 from 1967 until 1972. She now works for B.B.C. Television. Before joining the B.B.C., she worked as a research assistant at Nuffield College, Oxford. She is co-author with David Butler of the forthcoming edition of *British Political Facts* (Macmillan, 1973). She contributed a chapter on Cyprus to Evan Luard (ed.), *The International Regulation of Civil Wars* (Thames & Hudson, 1972).

Foreword

By Sir William Armstrong
Head of the Home Civil Service

Public understanding of the way in which our political institutions and governmental machinery work is crucial to the successful operation of democracy. Exposure of the machinery may not always led to admiration for its efficiency, and revelation may not always therefore be the natural first inclination of the civil servant or even the politician. But I firmly believe that, in some areas, both can benefit in their work if they are supported by the interest and informed scrutiny of the people.

British government departments and officials, who have featured prominently in the 'Talking Politics' series of radio programmes which comprise this book, have a reasonably good, and steadily improving, record of *giving* information to the public. But that is not quite the same thing as allowing information to be *extracted* – and broadcast. When I was first asked to assist in this enterprise, by suggesting areas worth exploring and participating myself, I was at pains to emphasise the distinction between, on the one hand, a civil servant's explaining what was done and the considerations affecting his advice and, on the other, his becoming involved in controversy over the nature of the decision or the advice itself.

Thanks to the sympathetic handling of both subject-matter and participants by Professor Anthony King and Anne Sloman, I think that this attempt to look beyond the day-to-day controversies of party politics and to examine in depth the features of our political system – rather than just taking them at face value – has been an outstanding success. Civil servants have found here an opportunity to describe their work and their roles – to explain 'how the wheels go round' – and I hope that audiences, too, have found it interesting.

In my view, perhaps the most significant contribution of this series to the cause of more public information has been to provide the sort of forum in which it is possible for both civil servants and politicians to be involved together in lively discussion of their work without either side breaking the 'rules', written and unwritten, which govern their behaviour.

I congratulate the B.B.C. in having devised a successful format which enabled the listener – and will enable the reader of this volume – to understand how some of our institutions work, and how and why particular governmental decisions come to be taken. I hope the programmes have helped to destroy the myth of 'facelessness' and to promote more confidence in 'openness'. If they have also provided the student of politics – all of us at one time or another – with a few practical illustrations to supplement the many standard works on theory, then I think they have been amply justified. For civil servants there will always be problems involved in appearing on public platforms, and areas of reticence which they must preserve, particularly in confidential advice to ministers. The line is difficult to draw, but, given goodwill on both sides and the common objective of public enlightenment, the attempt can and should continue to be made.

William Armstrong

Introduction

This is a somewhat unusual book, and the reader deserves to be told a little about its history. Every Saturday morning when Parliament is sitting, B.B.C. Radio 4 broadcasts a half-hour programme called 'The Week at Westminster'. The programme reviews the previous week's debates in Parliament, with discussion and comment by M.P.s and journalists. 'The Week at Westminster' is replaced during parliamentary recesses sometimes by special programmes, for example on the major party conferences, but usually by an *ad hoc* series called 'Talking Politics'. This book consists of the transcripts of eleven of the programmes broadcast in the 'Talking Politics' series over the past two years, with the addition of another radio documentary, 'Women in Parliament'. All twelve programmes were produced by Anne Sloman. Anthony King organised the material, wrote the scripts, and presented the programmes on the air.

The authors' chief purpose in preparing the series was this. Most of the political news on radio and television, and most of the political coverage in the newspapers, is concerned with current controversy – usually partisan controversy. The stuff of political news is the stuff of current politics: industrial relations, housing, immigration, incomes policy, or whatever. And this is as it should be. It is right that the public should know what problems are currently exercising Government and which of the Government's actions (or inactions) are open to criticism.

The day-to-day coverage in the news media is, however, apt to give a somewhat misleading impression of what Members of Parliament and Governments are like, and of how they go about their work – misleading in at least three ways. In the first place, much of what M.P.s and Governments do is not reported in the media at all. For example, most Members of Parliament spend a large proportion of their time – sometimes as much as a third or a half of it – performing services for their constituents, mainly on a person-to-person basis. A little of what M.P.s do in this connection is reported in the local press, but almost none of it is reported in the national press, and the great bulk of it is not reported at all. Many members of the general public are probably quite unaware of it. This was one of the gaps in people's knowledge that the series was trying to fill, especially in the first three of the programmes reprinted below.

In the second place, the emphasis that the media place – perfectly properly – on the elements in politics that are controversial is apt to give the impression that politics is concerned only with controversy and that all politics is party politics. This is not so. Much of what M.P.s do they do irrespective of party; a good deal of parliamentary work, some on the floor of the House of Commons but much more in committee, is conducted on a non-partisan basis; and of course most day-to-day administration proceeds regardless of which Government is in power. Several of the programmes in the series – notably 'A Select Committee at Work' and 'A Bill is Passed' – were designed to bring out this non-partisan element in political life. Reasonable men are shown in these programmes differing reasonably. Differences of opinion, even where they exist, are not always stridently expressed.

In the third place, political coverage in the media is apt to be misleading simply because it is hard to follow: journalists and broadcasters, deeply immersed as they are in the world of politics and government, often fail to remember that their readers and listeners may not fully understand what is meant by even such familiar phrases as 'three-line whip' or 'second reading'. Even if they do remember, they seldom have time to explain: no one wants every thirty-second news flash turned into a mini civics lecture. The 'Talking Politics' series was not concerned with giving civics lectures either; but it did seek, in passing, to provide the listener with a background of information against which day-to-day political news could be more readily comprehended. It also sought to provide the student of politics with the kind of concrete detail that is often missing from textbooks.

The programmes were originally broadcast over a period of two years and at fairly wide intervals: two or three at Christmas, one or two at Easter, and so on. They were not originally intended to form a coherent whole; but in time a certain coherence did emerge, and to some degree was consciously sought. The theme of the series is suggested by the title of the book *Westminster and Beyond*. The aim was to focus on the Member of Parliament and his working environment. The first four programmes below deal with the M.P. in relation to his constituency – his work on behalf of his constituents, and how he was originally selected as a candidate by his local constituency party or association. The fifth, 'Women in Parliament', deals with the position of women in the House of Commons. The next two are concerned with those whose job it is to report and comment on the doings of M.P.s: the Westminster lobby correspondents, and interviewers on television and radio. And the last five deal with the M.P. in his chief place of work, the Palace of Westminster itself – with debates on the floor of the House of Commons, with Question Time, with committees, and so on. The programmes' coverage is reasonably comprehensive, but the reader should be aware that certain subjects that might have been touched on were not. For instance, there is no programme on an M.P.'s relationship with his constituency party or association after he has been selected as a candidate, and none on adjournment debates or Private Members' Bills. These subjects were omitted, not because they are unimportant, but through force of circumstance.

There is another aspect of the series, however, that is worth drawing attention to. Five of the twelve programmes involved the active participation of Clerks to the House of Commons and civil servants. Civil servants, indeed, appeared in all the programmes that in any way bore on their work. It may sound obvious that they should appear, since so little of the work of government could, or does, go on without them; but, as Sir William Armstrong says in his Foreword, it is something quite new in British practice for civil servants, not merely to dispense information of the Government's or their own choosing, but to be questioned in detail about their participation in the taking of actual decisions – and to be questioned in the same context, about the same decisions, as their political masters. The series will have served a useful purpose if it conveys to the reader a realistic sense of the important roles that civil servants play, and if it encourages the Government to allow civil servants to speak in public more freely than in the past.

The technique of the series was simple enough, though there were often considerable practical difficulties. Two of the programmes – 'The Art of the Political Interviewer' and 'Debates on the Floor' – were straightforward discussion programmes ranging over a wide variety of topics and involving a number of persons brought together in a broadcasting studio. The other ten were documentaries, which attempted to make general points by focusing on a specific episode or on a few specific individuals. M.P.s, ministers, civil servants and members of the general public were interviewed in their offices or their homes or in broadcasting studios. The interviews were recorded and the main task of producer and presenter, as in all such cases, was to create an intelligible half-hour radio programme out of, often, hours of tape.

The main limitation of this technique should be apparent. Quite apart from the obvious danger of the tape's being edited in such a way as to distort a person's meaning or to give a false impression of what actually happened in a particular situation, there is the more subtle danger that the episodes or individuals focused on will turn out to have been in some important way untypical. To take the first programme printed below, for example, on M.P.s' surgeries, it may be the case that other M.P.s conduct their surgeries in a manner quite unlike that of Shirley Williams or Norman Tebbit – or indeed (as is true in some cases) do not conduct surgeries at all. To take another example, 'A Select Committee at Work', it may be that other select committees carry out their duties in a style quite different from that of the Select Committee on Science and Technology. All one can do is alert the reader to this possibility and say that, whatever the outcome, the intention was to produce case-studies that were as typical as case-studies ever can be.

One final point. Most radio and television programmes about politics, and most books about politics, seek either to criticise or to justify. These programmes, and this book, seek for the most part merely to describe. Partly for this reason, and partly because the emphasis here is deliberately upon the non-partisan and the relatively non-controversial, the book as a whole may have a somewhat Panglossian air about it. It may give the impression that the authors believe that, in British politics, everything is for the best in this best of all possible worlds. They do not. They could equally well have produced a series of programmes highly critical of the same institutions and the same procedures that are here merely described. But they do believe that, logically, description should precede criticism and justification. They also believe that, if the general public knew more about British politicians and British political institutions, they would on the whole be more, not less, impressed by them. Familiarity in the case of the present authors has bred, not contempt, but considerable respect.

We should like to express our appreciation to the B.B.C. not only for allowing us to publish the transcripts of the programmes in book form, but, more important, for creating the atmosphere in which serious political programmes of this sort can be made. To the B.B.C.'s parliamentary staff, to our colleagues in Radio, and especially to the Editor of General Current Affairs, Stephen Bonarjee, all of whom have been consistently generous with advice and help, we owe a great debt.

It is the customary thing to say in acknowledgements to a book of this kind that, in spite of the enormous assistance given to the authors by X, Y, and Z, the views expressed are entirely the authors' own. The views expressed in this book, however, are not entirely our own: they are those of the ministers, Members of Parliament, party officials, civil servants, and members of the public who took part in the series, and we should like to thank them all, both for their interest and co-operation when we were recording the programmes, and subsequently for generously giving permission for their contributions to be published.

We should also like to record our gratitude to the many people who did not appear in the series but who nevertheless made a considerable indirect contribution to it: officials at the party headquarters, officials of the House of Commons, and members of that often maligned profession, the government information officers. In particular, we should like to break with precedent by thanking two civil servants by name: Sir William Armstrong, the Head of the Home Civil Service, who kindly agreed to write our Foreword and who has from the start encouraged our attempts to bring microphones into Whitehall; and Sydney Cursley, his Chief Information Officer, who was an unfailing source of support and practical advice.

Finally, we must thank two secretaries to the series,

Jacqueline Ward and Barbara Revill, who spent many dreary hours, often far into the night, transcribing the interviews from tape. It was not an easy job. They did it cheerfully, and exceedingly well.

A.K.
A.S.

1 M.P.s and their Surgeries

In the early eighteenth century, a particularly obstreperous Member of Parliament replied in these terms to some constituents who had written to him asking him to vote against the Budget. 'Gentlemen,' he said, 'I have received your letter about the excise and I am surprised at your insolence in writing to me at all. You know, and I know, that I bought this constituency. You know, and I know, that I am now determined to sell it, and you know what you think I don't know, that you are now looking out for another buyer, and I know what you certainly don't know, that I have now found another constituency to buy. About what you say about the excise. May God's curse light upon you all and may it make your homes as open and free to the excise officer as your wives and daughters have always been to me while I have represented your rascally constituency.'

In the 1970s Members of Parliament may occasionally feel that way about their constituents, but they certainly don't say so. For one thing, they have to win their seats in Parliament at the polls; they can't just buy them. For another, most M.P.s today do conscientiously feel that it's part of their job, not necessarily to agree with their constituents, but at least to listen to them and to do their best to serve them. And it's one of the means by which they serve them, the institution of the surgery – or the M.P.'s 'advice bureau', as it's sometimes called – that we're going to explore in this programme. Recently we spent two days visiting the surgeries of two Members of Parliament who sit for constituencies near London: Mrs Shirley Williams, the Labour M.P. for Hitchin in Hertfordshire, and Norman Tebbit, Conservative Member for Epping in Essex, not very far away. We recorded their surgeries, unrehearsed, with the permission of the people

---

Documentary broadcast on 8 April 1972.

who came along to them, and we talked to the two M.P.s about their surgery work. How often does Shirley Williams hold surgeries?

WILLIAMS: Twice in a month: at three towns on one Saturday and at two on the following Saturday, giving a fortnight in between; so every town in my constituency, of which there are five, has one surgery once a month.

KING: Norman Tebbit holds his a bit less often.

TEBBIT: I've precisely followed the example of my predecessor as the Member of Parliament for Epping and I hold my advice bureau on the first Saturday in every month. I think this is easy for people to remember and on that day I go to four centres in the constituency, Chingford, Waltham Abbey, Epping and Harlow, and spend all day on it.

KING: The idea of the surgery is very simple. The Member of Parliament announces that he or she will be available in the constituency at a particular time and at a particular place, and anyone is free to bring along whatever problems he has. Interviews between M.P.s and their constituents sometimes last only a minute or two, occasionally the best part of half an hour. Norman Tebbit had already held surgeries at Chingford and Waltham Abbey by the time we joined him after lunch in a local hall in Epping. There were four or five people waiting to see him when we arrived, and a local councillor sat in. The man at the head of the queue was actually bringing an invitation.

CONSTITUENT: I'm the publicity officer for the Coopersale Horticultural Society and we're holding our annual show in the local schoolroom on Saturday, 19 August, and the committee wondered if you would be kind enough to present the prizes after the show.

TEBBIT: I'm not quite certain when we shall be away on holiday; but I fancy that it's the week after that, so unless anything else is going to conflict with it, yes, certainly.

KING: But not many people come to an M.P.'s surgery bringing invitations. Most of them come with problems, sometimes pretty heart-rending problems. When we arrived at the new town of Harlow, just a few miles down the road from Epping, there was quite a queue waiting. One young man had brought along his wife and baby daughter, who sat peacefully during the whole interview. They were living with the wife's parents who'd given them a month to move out. The wife was pregnant. Would Mr Tebbit help get them a council house? They were getting desperate.

CONSTITUENT: You know. You can say I've got a month to go before the end of this month. But the father-in-law, you know, he's ill at the moment. He's at home all the time. All he does all day, sort of thing, is go on and on and on about the baby being in the way, one thing and another. By the end of the time he's finished being ill, we're either going to be out of a house or my wife's going to be a nervous wreck and she's going to end up having another . . . losing this other baby. She nearly lost it once, you know, and . . . her nerves are getting so bad. I come home some nights and she just cries her eyes out, on top of me, you know what I mean?

KING: Mr Tebbit promised to get in touch with the local housing officer to see if he could help, though beyond that there wasn't much he could do. In fact, although constituents bring their problems to their M.P.s, their representatives at Westminster, a very high proportion of the problems don't really concern *central* government at all, but *local* government. More than half of those who came to see Shirley Williams, for instance, raised things that fall squarely within the local authorities' province, a lot of them having to do with housing. Mrs Williams's surgery in the small town of Baldock is held in the hall of the Congregational Church, with rather spartan wooden benches and one of those old-fashioned pastel-tinted pictures of Jesus leading the children on the wall. A lady in her mid-fifties had come, at first rather shyly, to complain that for six years she'd been trying to get the local council to re-wire her house.

CONSTITUENT: Because we can't have an electric fire anywhere in the house. There are no plugs in the bedrooms or anything and they said that that was needed to be done immediately, and that's six years ago and I go every week and they won't do a thing about it, and yet, when somebody moves out from their house, they re-wire it straight away before anybody else gets in, and we have to pay the rent, and every time the rent goes up we have to pay more and get nothing done.

KING: To her M.P. the next move was clear.

WILLIAMS: It would be a good idea if you were to call in at

the council offices yourself next week and make a formal complaint. In fact, I would write a letter and deliver it by hand at the same time, and then I can write for you, but it would be helpful if you made application yourself, first. So don't just rely on chatting to the foreman, go up and put in a formal complaint. All right?

KING: Shirley Williams ran into another straight council case at Royston, where she holds her surgery in one of the committee rooms in the town hall. Someone came to complain that he simply couldn't get a planning decision out of the local council. He owned a local hotel and now wanted planning permission to run a restaurant for non-residents as well. All he said he wanted out of the council was a decision. Could he open the restaurant or couldn't he?

WILLIAMS: And you want a decision as soon as possible. . . .

CONSTITUENT: Yes. Responsible people in the town think I'm telling lies when I say all the decision is about is whether or not I can serve you a meal without you sleeping the night.

WILLIAMS: Well, of course, it's a different licence but we'll see what we can do anyway. So, I'll have a go. . . .

KING: And having a go at the council is what M.P.s following up their surgeries spend a good deal of time doing. Ordinary citizens tend to turn to their Member of Parliament because they're not quite sure who deals with what in government, and often the local authority just doesn't seem to be listening. The M.P. doesn't have any formal power over local authorities, of course, but since he is an M.P. he's bound to be paid attention to. Norman Tebbit puts it this way.

TEBBIT: An awful lot of them are housing problems. I think this is something that's common to most of us, or problems of dealing with bureaucracy, that people just can't cope with. They can't get into the bureaucracy at the right level, whereas, as I explained to them, I have no particular power, but I do write from a terribly good address, which ensures that the letter is answered by somebody fairly senior.

KING: Many M.P.s hold their surgeries in their local party headquarters, but all the five we visited were in council offices, church halls, and suchlike. Does Shirley Williams ever hold them on the premises of the Labour Party?

WILLIAMS: I think the real truth of the matter is that we've only got one set of premises in those five towns, but I don't on the whole. I try to hold it in the council offices or the town hall because I think it should be seen as a kind of civic service rather than as a purely political exercise.

KING: And Norman Tebbit takes the same view.

TEBBIT: I refuse absolutely to use party premises because I think it could be embarrassing for someone who's a committed Labour voter; after all, sometimes a Labour councillor has a personal problem he comes to me with, and he wouldn't want to be seen coming into my party headquarters, and I wouldn't want an agent, a party agent, to have anything to do with this side of my life. It's outside politics what I do on these days.

KING: Some of the problems that constituents bring don't involve a great deal of follow-up – the writing of one letter, maybe a couple – but some of them consume a lot of time. The problem that one lady presented to Norman Tebbit was, in essence, fairly simple; but from his reply you can imagine how much time he thought he was going to have to put into it.

CONSTITUENT: I teach in the convent in Bishops Stortford and I teach five periods, four mornings a week, which is twenty periods a week out of forty, and Hertfordshire County Council, instead of paying me for half, they pay me four-tenths. They look upon the day as two sessions, two equal sessions, you see, whereas it's eight periods of five in the morning, three in the afternoon.

TEBBIT: Is it the same, do you know, in other education authorities?

CONSTITUENT: Oh, no. In no other, I don't think, and certainly not in Essex.

TEBBIT: Now, you really do disappoint me, because I'm always holding Hertfordshire up as being a more progressive educational authority than Essex.

CONSTITUENT: But this is so iniquitous, that one is paid exactly the same whether one teaches for three and a half or two hours.

TEBBIT: I'll take it up first of all with the Education Officer so that I've got, in writing, his view and then presumably he will stick to his present brief and from there I'll go to the chairman of the educational authority. What I'll also do, of course, is to have a word with Essex Education Authority to make sure that they don't take the same view.

CONSTITUENT: No, they don't. . . .

TEBBIT: And if they take your view, which I understand they do, then I'll use this as part of the ammunition. I always try and play them off one against the other.

KING: At a minimum it sounded as though that case, even though a fairly simple one, was going to demand at least three letters, maybe a dozen telephone calls. Shirley Williams tells us that she's already written no less than thirty-seven letters arising out of the surgeries we recorded, Norman Tebbit between twenty-five and thirty. In fact, the first person Mrs Williams saw in the Council of Social Service offices in Letchworth was clearly going to take up a great deal of time and did raise rather complicated issues. She was an East African Asian, soft-spoken, wearing a lovely mauve sari, with a good command of English. She was having trouble training to become a teacher in England. She'd been to see Mrs Williams before.

CONSTITUENT: Remember last time I visited you, I informed you that my training wasn't recognised here, and it was suggested that I take up a training course at one of the colleges. So I sent in my application to the various colleges, and I have had replies from two of the colleges saying that I can't be given a grant as I haven't lived here for three years. My whole career is ruined. It's fifteen years of my teaching experience, plus a year that I've already put in, and I think my case should be considered in some way or other.

WILLIAMS: The first thing we need to do is to make sure that you're offered a place. If you're offered a place I will attempt to get you a grant as a special case and I think I may succeed; but the important thing is that I must be able to say, to the county council, that you have been offered a place in a college.

CONSTITUENT: They cannot offer me a place because I haven't stayed here for three years. That's the regulation.

WILLIAMS: There's nothing to stop a college accepting you although you have not been here for three years. Any college can accept you. If you're accepted by a college, then I can see if we can get you a discretionary grant. So what I would suggest you do – *you* do. I'll do the other side of it – is ring up or write to the Clearing House and ask them if your application can be left in for colleges although you've not been here for three years. Say you want to go ahead in spite of no certainty of a grant.

KING: You heard Shirley Williams say that she'd do her bit if the lady who'd come to see her would do hers, and probably most M.P.s are readiest to help those who show the most signs of wanting to help themselves. The only time in a long morning when Mrs Williams began to get a bit irritated was with a long-winded lady who was a good deal more anxious to talk than to listen.

CONSTITUENT: I was here the last time, you remember, and I never got nothing, never received nothing off them. The income tax? I didn't get anything. I went to the unemployment and got this this morning off them, 'cos I don't get any benefit until next week, but regards that, they told me yesterday that Bruce can claim income tax for me.

WILLIAMS: Now, I'm quite willing to write to try to get you some help, but I can't do things unless you help me, too, and I can't make an appeal for you. There's no way I can do it.

CONSTITUENT: The point is, this is what I'm getting at. I'm Mr Page's common law wife.

WILLIAMS: Right.

CONSTITUENT: Right?

WILLIAMS: Yes.

CONSTITUENT: He can't claim tax for me and he's on the insurance; he can't claim for me if I'm not working either. This £5 is supposed to keep the two of us. They have £2·10 off of that for maintenance for his ex-wife. Now, now tell us the truth. Now, I have known them. . . . [etc., etc.].

KING: And of course some people who come along to surgeries are just a nuisance. Shirley Williams has one constituent who's been attending her surgery in Baldock every month for at least the last two years. He's convinced he was wrongly convicted of a motoring offence.

CONSTITUENT: Is there any progress from your point of view?

WILLIAMS: I've written you a letter which you should have got. The councillor in East Suffolk says he has not sent any evidence to the Luton and Bedfordshire Constabulary and, indeed, he doesn't think there's any case of perjury involved.

CONSTITUENT: The transcript of the evidence shows that and proves it. The statements from the police, I have here.

WILLIAMS: Yes, that's an old friend, that one. The trouble is that nobody agrees with you, you see.

KING: You might have thought that M.P.s would try to set up some sort of screening procedure to separate out the serious cases from others and the ones they really can deal with from the ones they can't. But Norman Tebbit and Shirley Williams, and most other M.P.s we've talked to, are opposed to this sort of thing. Norman Tebbit said flatly:

TEBBIT: I see anybody that comes. If we get really pushed, and sometimes we do at Harlow, then I may ask a councillor to make some notes of it beforehand, if possible, to help me get through more quickly; but basically this is the day of the month when, if anyone wants to talk to me about anything, they can.

KING: And Shirley Williams is of the same view.

WILLIAMS: I've got an assistant who is very useful in that, particularly if we have a very heavy surgery, he will see some people in advance to discover whether their cases are basically local authority or not, and if we're really pushed I will then ask the councillor to see the local authority cases on his own.

KING: In London last year someone kept track of the number of people visiting a particular M.P.'s surgery each week and reckoned that this particular M.P. saw a minimum of one hundred and twenty people a year. Norman Tebbit and Shirley Williams both see far more, mainly because they represent constituencies that are, in population terms, amongst the largest in the country. Shirley Williams talked to seventeen constituents the day we were there and, if that's a typical day, which she said it was, that works out at something like, not one hundred and twenty people in a year, but nearer three hundred and sixty. How do people find their way to an M.P.'s surgery? We asked a shopkeeper who attended Norman Tebbit's advice bureau.

CONSTITUENT: Well, this morning I was working in the shop and I was serving someone with a sports bag. They took it on approval and as I took the name and address of the person down – it's funny – it rang a bell that this person was the wife of a councillor. I raised this problem with this person and they said, well, the bureau's open this afternoon. I'd been meaning to come down before but I never got round to it as I work Saturday afternoons normally, but I just took an hour off to nip down and sort it all out.

KING: But he could equally well have looked in his local paper, where most M.P.s advertise their surgeries – like this young Jamaican.

CONSTITUENT: It's always in the paper when Mrs Williams is coming and I read the local paper and this is how I know about it.

KING: The shopkeeper's problem and the young Jamaican's, like so many others, had to do with local government. One of them wanted something done about local parking arrangements, the other help with compensation on a house that had been demolished by the Greater London Council. But, of course, not everybody who comes to an M.P.'s surgery wants something taken up with a local authority. Many of the cases concern claims for pensions or supplementary benefit, which are the responsibility of central government. And a few people, a very few, actually do want to discuss great matters of national policy.

CONSTITUENT: Now, the thing that I want to know about the Common Market is: how much are we going to pay for entering this Common Market? I mean, in cash over the next ten years.

WILLIAMS: The British contribution to the budget is about 22 per cent. The European . . . the size of the European budget is not yet decided, and won't be decided for . . . [etc., etc.].

KING: Norman Tebbit had one caller, the chairman of the women's section of one of the local Conservative associations, who came to take him to task because she thought the Government wasn't right-wing enough. Why weren't they tougher with the I.R.A.? And what about their attitude towards that other major national political issue – albeit in a local government context – education?

CONSTITUENT: They're absolutely unanimously against comprehensive schooling, and we went to a meeting in Theydon Bois last year, and an Essex County Council lady spoke to us and she said it was in the pipeline. Well, they were in an uproar, they just didn't want it. Why are we having it planted on us when we don't want it? I mean, we worked hard enough to get the councillors and the M.P.s in, and I think we should have a say. I mean, why should we have it?

TEBBIT: Well, my answer to that is that you shouldn't really.

CONSTITUENT: No.

TEBBIT: And to put the record straight, at the moment it is, of course, a county council responsibility – education – and how they reorganise it. Still, in this area, in Epping itself, the children still are selected at eleven, and those who are selected as being 'suitable for a course of academic instruction' – in the words that they use – have a chance of getting to a selective school, such as a grammar school, yes. Unfortunately, there are now not enough places to accommodate the children that pass. My own daughter, for example, last year passed her eleven-plus, but there was no place for her, and she's at Ongar Comprehensive. So I feel as you do. I'd like to see more selective places available. My own daughter is affected in this matter, but it is the County Council who made this decision.

CONSTITUENT: Well, I mean, it . . . it's a down grade, isn't it, I mean lumping them together?

TEBBIT: I am inclined to agree with you in many cases, not all. I think, for example, to have a comprehensive school at Waltham Abbey was a right decision.

CONSTITUENT: Yes . . . certain areas.

TEBBIT: There are right places for it and wrong places for it. But it seems that – whether I'm in a minority or not I don't know – Essex County Council is making its own decision, and what I do suggest is that you have a go at your county councillors.

KING: Perhaps surprisingly, quite a lot of the problems constituents bring to their M.P.s don't really concern *government* at all – central or local. One of the people who come to see Norman Tebbit in Harlow was in a state of considerable distress. He'd worked for a particular firm for twenty years, but had then had an accident which kept him off sick for several months. When he returned to work he found that the firm had proposed to his union that he be declared redundant.

CONSTITUENT: Now I don't know anything about this. I was just called in on 3 September, before one of the directors, and he told me he was putting me off on a month's notice. So I said when he'd finished: 'Mr Eliot,' I said, 'I reject everything you have said. Now,' I said, 'I will make no decisions, only through my solicitor and my union.' And on 10 September I was put off. I've approached my union several times and they are not prepared to take any action as far as I know. As a matter of fact they are now going as far as trying to get me out of the union as far as I can see. I think I have the last letter, which looks to me that this is what the secretary means in this little bit now.

TEBBIT: I don't think they're pushing you out of the union. I think they're moving your papers to their London office. I'll write about your case, if I may, to the union.

CONSTITUENT: Yes.

TEBBIT: And we'll get it absolutely clear from them what's going on.

CONSTITUENT: Yes.

TEBBIT: Because they can't just chuck you out of the union, it seems to me. I'm sure the rules don't allow them to chuck you out, without really good cause.

CONSTITUENT: Yes. I mean to say, what chance have I got of going outside and getting a job if the firm where I worked for twenty years can't give me a job?

TEBBIT: Yes . . . yes, I . . . I understand. Yes, I think I'd better take copies of some of these letters for my own file, and look carefully at them before I decide just how I write to the union and to the company.

KING: Two of the problems brought to Shirley Williams the morning we were in Hertfordshire, which also had nothing to do with government in the strict sense, concerned litigation. In both cases her constituents wanted her to approach their solicitors and, if need be, the Law Society. Both were complaining that they'd been overcharged.

CONSTITUENT: I'd better fill you in with a few details for a start. This involves a problem of a dispute between myself and my brother over the estate that my mother left when she died. In fact, she left money and a house. Well, my brother shared the money with me, but he kept quiet about the house. This didn't come to light until quite a long time afterwards.

KING: The dispute eventually went to court, though in the meantime the constituent's brother had died. The judge ruled that the house did indeed belong to Mrs Williams's constituent, and that the sale of the house should go to cover costs, which came altogether to £850. But the constituent reckoned the house, in the condition it was in, would only fetch about that sum. So he and his wife and two friends spent a week fixing it up. And in the end he sold it for nearly £1,300, and his solicitors congratulated him on making a profit.

CONSTITUENT: Then comes the bombshell. I wrote to this firm of solicitors and asked them when this matter was going to be settled up, because the court case was in November and we're still playing around. In his letter he says the court costs are now over £1,000 – so, we've had a jump of £500.

KING: Mrs Williams's constituent felt he'd had no explanation of why his costs had doubled and he'd received no detailed bill.

WILLIAMS: Did you ever have a letter, or anything of that kind, mentioning £500, or was that just what the judge said?

CONSTITUENT: That was what was said in court.

WILLIAMS: In court. Fine. Well, what I'll do is write to your solicitors and ask them to let you have straight away a detailed breakdown of the costs. When we've got that, we can then take it up with the Law Society. In fact, on reflection I think really, Mr Hollingsworth, you ought to write to them and ask for a detailed breakdown of the costs, and if you don't get a reply within ten days let me know at the House of Commons. I'll then write if they haven't replied to you. If they do reply, send me the letter at the House of Commons and we'll take it from there. I'll take it up with the Law Society.

KING: So at least two M.P.s, it seems, are prepared to follow up cases that aren't strictly governmental, within reason. And according to Shirley Williams the number of people bringing such cases is pretty large.

WILLIAMS: Quite a lot, maybe one in five. And they will vary. A lot of them would be about troubles with private firms, or private house-building firms or something of that kind. Some would be purely personal, people wanting to get what you might describe as advice that would come better from a trained social worker, perhaps, than from me.

KING: Members of Parliament can help their constituents in all sorts of ways. As Norman Tebbit says, the House of Commons is a terribly good address. They can write letters and make phone calls, they can go and see people if necessary. They can call on ministers, ask Questions in the House of Commons, and refer matters to the Ombudsman. Their great strength lies in the fact that they know more about how the system works than almost anybody else. But how often, out of all the people who come to see them, do they really feel they've managed to accomplish something? Norman Tebbit.

TEBBIT: A very difficult question. In the sense of helping, I think one can probably help most of them, because some of them really want to come and talk about something which is a problem which is absolutely insoluble, and which they know is absolutely insoluble in some cases. But, as to arriving at a satisfactory solution to the problem, I think perhaps as many as a third in the long run, although sometimes it is a very long run before one solves it.

KING: Shirley Williams's proportions aren't so very different.

WILLIAMS: Well, totally succeed perhaps one time in four. Partially succeed in perhaps half of the cases. I wouldn't reckon that more than a quarter would be dead failures.

KING: Both Mrs Williams and Mr Tebbit admit to being depressed occasionally by some of the particularly sad stories – true stories – they find themselves listening to. And perhaps the nastiest aspect of the job is facing the fact that, however much you'd like to help, sometimes you just can't.

TEBBIT: I honestly don't know how we can help in this matter, because, as you know, there's not enough housing in Harlow at the moment, even for the companies who are sponsoring people. The only thing honestly that I am able to do about this at all is to go on kicking the Minister to tell him that we've got to expand Harlow and we've got to build more houses here, which is not very much comfort to you.

KING: If it takes up so much time, if M.P.s have to write so many letters, if they sometimes find the work depressing, why do almost all Members of Parliament hold surgeries? The cynic would say 'in order to win votes, of course'. But the cynic would be wrong. There is no evidence that this sort of careful individual constituency work makes any substantial difference at the time of a general election, and M.P.s know it. I asked Shirley Williams how far she thought her surgery work helped her win the allegiance of the voters.

WILLIAMS: I don't think that it makes much difference. All you can say is that perhaps you gradually build up a reputation as a conscientious or reasonably hard-working M.P., and that is of some advantage. But with the individual cases I suspect there's almost no influence at all.

KING: How much advantage – hundreds of votes, thousands?

WILLIAMS: At most, hundreds.

KING: Norman Tebbit seemed surprised even to be asked. Had he won any votes that morning?

TEBBITT: Do you know I've never thought of it? I can't say that for me the favourite part of my life as a Member of Parliament is being a social worker, which is what one is on these occasions. But I just regard it as part of my job and, as to whether it wins votes or not, you know, I'm not really particularly interested. I don't particularly want to win votes about these sort of things, because, I think, I, my predecessor, and whoever follows me will do this job in much the same way.

KING: But perhaps the most important thing about M.P.s' surgeries isn't the help that M.P.s are able to give to, after all, a fairly limited number of individuals. What their surgeries do is give Members of Parliament, who could so easily become completely immersed in the rarefied atmosphere of Westminster, some sense of how the decisions taken by government really affect the day-to-day lives of ordinary people – some sense, as they say, of where the shoe pinches. In its modest way the M.P.'s surgery is one of the most important means we have in our system for ensuring that our governors don't get too far out of touch with the governed.

2 The Case of Flora Ginetio

Most of us, when we think of politics, probably think instinctively of party politics – of sharp differences of opinion, slanging matches, point-scoring, and so on. Most of us, too, when we hear about Members of Parliament, probably think of the House of Commons itself and of the debates that go on there. But a great deal of politics doesn't involve the parties at all, and a lot of the work of an M.P. doesn't really have much to do with standing up and making speeches in the House; it goes on whether Parliament is in recess or not. These are important facts about the system of government we have in Britain, and this programme, like the one on M.P.s' surgeries, is meant to illustrate them. We are going to illustrate them in this case by telling a story – a simple story in itself, an interesting one, and we think an important one. Our story involves a Birmingham housewife, a girl from Italy, a Member of Parliament, two ministers, and three civil servants. It is a true story, and of course it has a happy ending.

It all began last autumn. Every fortnight Roy Hattersley, the M.P. for the Sparkbrook Division of Birmingham, holds two surgeries in different parts of his constituency. That is, he does the same as most M.P.s: he makes himself available at a particular time, and people are free to come along to him with their problems. His visitor one September morning was Mrs Iris Whitehouse, the wife of an inspector in a Birmingham car factory. What was the problem she put to him?

WHITEHOUSE: That we had an Italian girl living with us who had been coming for a number of years, and she wanted to stay in this country, and she'd got to find employment, which she did do. And that she was told that, if she could find employment, she

---

Documentary broadcast on 17 April 1971.

would be given a work permit to stay in the country. She got the employment. We applied for the work permit, and it was refused.

KING: So you were asking Roy Hattersley to find some means whereby she could be allowed to stay in the country?

WHITEHOUSE: Yes.

KING: The girl's name was Flora Ginetio. She was twenty years old. She had no real family in Italy, she had lived most of her life in children's homes of one sort and another, and long before last autumn she had come to think of the Whitehouses' modest semi-detached home in Acocks Green, Birmingham, as her only home. And Mr and Mrs Whitehouse, who already had a daughter of their own, also thought of Flora as a real member of the family. How had all this happened?

WHITEHOUSE: Well, a number of years ago, at the school my daughter was attending, the headmistress asked one day if any family would be prepared to give a summer holiday to deprived children in foreign countries. We said we would, and Flora was the child who came to us from Italy. And from that time she came yearly for a summer holiday when possible. When she was seventeen, she was allowed to stay for nine months. Then she had to leave the country because she wasn't allowed to take up employment. She finally returned to us last year, in July, hoping to stay and take up employment. And that is when the trouble started.

KING: In Italy Flora had worked for a time helping to look after mentally retarded children. She liked the work and wanted, if possible, to do the same kind of thing in Britain. And she was lucky, or so she thought. She was offered a position caring for children at the Warwick House Short Stay Unit, run by the Birmingham Public Health Department. But then, as Mrs Whitehouse says, the Department of Employment would not give her a work permit. Why not? We asked Bill Winter, the Department's Midlands Regional Controller.

WINTER: She had been allowed originally into the country as a visitor and, when she made the application, my headquarters found that it was a non-residential job and, as things were, they rejected the application on those grounds.

KING: So there it was. The Warwick House job was not a living-in job. Therefore, no work permit. And worse was to follow. Mrs Whitehouse went to see Roy Hattersley in the first place because Flora had been given a fortnight to leave the country.

WHITEHOUSE: That's right, yes. We received a letter from the Home Office in which they said that, as the Department of Employment and Productivity cannot agree to your employment with the City of Birmingham Public Health Department, you should either forward to this department an alternative offer of employment or make arrangements to leave the United Kingdom.

KING: What did Mrs Whitehouse think her Member of Parliament could do for her when she went to see him?

WHITEHOUSE: Well, we were sure that somehow he would be able to help us and that, if he couldn't help us, no one could.

KING: Why did you go and see your M.P.? After all, you might have written a letter to the local paper; you might have got in touch with the Home Office yourself.

WHITEHOUSE: Well, it was an instinctive reaction in the family, I think, that we should go to our local M.P., who we thought could help.

KING: Roy Hattersley thought he could help – mainly because he and other M.P.s have to deal with cases like this all the time. But what about this one? When Mrs Whitehouse first told him about Flora, did he think this was a particularly striking case, or was it fairly routine?

HATTERSLEY: Well, in one sense all cases are fairly routine in that one has twenty or thirty every week. Indeed, one is sitting there four times a month waiting for cases. But in another sense it was more than routine. There was an orphan girl who wanted to do some very important social work in Britain, who had the chance of living with a British family and being, one hopes, happy for the next fifteen, twenty or thirty years, and one little bit of bureaucracy was stopping that from happening. And it seemed rather important to destroy that bit of bureaucracy.

KING: Roy Hattersley's first move was to write to the Foreign Office to get an extension on Flora's permission to stay in the country. Within a day or two his letter was on the desk of one of the Foreign Office ministers, Anthony Royle, the Parliamentary Under-Secretary. And it was Anthony Royle who replied. We asked him how many letters of this sort he got from M.P.s about constituents' complaints.

ROYLE: Well, I get quite a number. I knew you were going to ask me this question. I've done some investigation and I discover that over the last four and a half months I've had somewhere in the region of a hundred and twenty. It varies of course from month to month and week to week.

KING: The draft answers to the letters ministers get from M.P.s are prepared by civil servants. But how often does someone like Anthony Royle look at a letter and think 'No, I don't think that's quite right' and send it back to have changes made?

ROYLE: Oh, quite, quite often. The original drafts are produced by officials in the office and submitted to me, and with the draft comes the file with all the background information on which this draft is based, and I read this extremely carefully. Most of the people one is writing back to are colleagues in the House of Commons who I know personally, like for instance I know Roy Hattersley personally, and I believe that it is not only courteous but very important that ministers should take great personal interest in the background to each case, and there are many cases that come to me which I send back, when I'm not satisfied with the draft, which are redrafted, and then I add on personal comments of my own.

KING: But there is one further point. As it happens, Roy Hattersley is a Labour Member of Parliament, indeed an Opposition spokesman on foreign affairs. Anthony Royle is a Conservative Foreign Office minister. Does it make any difference to Anthony Royle whether the M.P. who writes to him is on his own side?

ROYLE: Not at all. I'm not interested what the party of the Member is. I write back on the facts of the case, and the question of whether he's a Labour Member or a Liberal Member or a Conservative Member doesn't really come into it. People when they become Members of Parliament act on behalf of all their constituents whatever their party politics, and as a minister who is writing back to a Member of Parliament who is approaching the minister on behalf of his constituents, again the fact of party affiliation doesn't enter into it.

KING: The funny thing, though, was that in writing to the Foreign Office Roy Hattersley had inadvertently written to the wrong department. He should have got in touch with the Home Office, which deals with immigration and nationality matters. How did he happen to do this?

HATTERSLEY: Simple mistake. I believed the initial application for an immigrant to come into this country, assuming that they're not Commonwealth immigrants, was taken by the Foreign Office, and I frankly wrote to the wrong department.

KING: But it was not a serious mistake, since the Foreign Office simply passed the letter on to the Home Office and said that Mr Hattersley could expect to hear from them. And from this point onwards the main characters in our story are civil servants. Constitutionally, almost all decisions taken by government departments are taken in the name of, and on behalf of, ministers of the Crown. But of course ministers do not begin to have the time to look in detail at every case. They have to rely on the experience and good judgement of their permanent officials. It is the permanent officials who go into the cases in detail and make recommendations to their political masters. The civil servant on whose desk Flora's file eventually arrived was John Hamilton, a Senior Principal in the Home Office's Immigration and Nationality Department. We talked to Mr Hamilton in his office in Holborn. By what route had the file reached his desk?

HAMILTON: Well, it arrived on my desk after going through a number of offices. Mr Hattersley, as you know, wrote to the Foreign Secretary in the first instance, but since the subject was not one for the Foreign Secretary or his department, the private office of the Foreign Office sent the correspondence to the private office of the Home Office Secretary of State.

KING: The private office being the minister's own personal staff.

HAMILTON: Being the minister's own personal staff, where it would be sorted out as being a matter for the Immigration and Nationality Department to advise and present the facts. The papers would then come to the Immigration and Nationality Department, where the file of Flora would be found from where it would be resting in our registry; and the whole case would then be considered at what one might call an intermediate level and submitted to me for onward transmission to the Minister of State with a recommendation.

KING: When the file did arrive on your desk, what roughly was in it?

HAMILTON: Obviously there is the correspondence from Mr Hattersley to the Foreign Secretary and the replies which had been sent on behalf of the Foreign Secretary. But there is also our own file on Flora, which goes back some years since she first came here under the auspices of the organisation for helping children. And the subsequent visits that she paid here were all noted and recorded in her file. So that we did have considerable evidence about her background and her association with someone in this country.

KING: On the basis of this information, Mr Hamilton decided that, at the very least, Flora could be allowed to stay in Britain until the end of last year. The reason was that . . .

HAMILTON: . . . she had in fact been invited to submit another offer of employment which the Department of Employment might approve. But, as she had not done so, it seemed reasonable to me against the background of her connection with an English family for many years that she had a safe home here for a time and could be allowed a reasonable time in which to, perhaps, find employment which the Department of Employment could approve.

KING: Who actually took the decision? Yourself or Lord Windlesham, the minister?

HAMILTON: Intrinsically, it must be Lord Windlesham who took the decision, although I should say that, if the case had come to me to deal with in the ordinary way, I would have taken exactly the same decision and I would, in fact, have taken the decision myself.

KING: In the event, Mr Hamilton drafted a letter for Lord Windlesham which Lord Windlesham signed and sent off to Roy Hattersley. It said that Flora was being given an extension and suggested that she get in touch with the local office of the Department of Employment in Birmingham. At this point Roy Hattersley could have done either of two things. He could have given Flora news of the extension and, as far as getting a job was concerned, left her to get on with it; or he could get in touch with the Department of Employment on her behalf. He chose to do the latter, but this time, instead of writing to the minister, Robert Carr, he wrote directly to the Midlands Regional Controller, Mr Winter, a civil servant. We asked him why.

HATTERSLEY: Well, for two reasons. One was that I knew Winter, I knew Winter very well, and the second was that we wanted things to move quickly. I knew Winter because I had been minister in the department in which he served, and it's very sensible, I think, if one knows a local official: one has some rapport with him and one is able to talk with him on much more friendly terms than writing to the rather faceless, and rather amorphous, central ministry in Whitehall.

KING: Bill Winter, as Regional Controller, is in charge of a huge organisation covering the whole of the Midlands. He could hardly be expected to help Flora find a job himself. So he did the natural thing: he arranged for her to go and see Mr Bob Cook, the manager of the employment exchange for the Small Heath part of Birmingham where the Whitehouses live. Bob Cook takes up the story.

COOK: The first thing was to find out if we had any details about Miss Ginetio. We hadn't in fact. And we were asked, knowing what had previously happened, whether there were any other suitable vacancies possible for her to take. At that particular moment there were two possibilities. We wrote to her asking her to come in and see us and discuss this. Well, she did so, but some little time later, by which time the matron thought that the vacancy had been filled; this was subject to the selected candidate passing a medical examination. So there was nothing more to be done. A couple of days later we asked the children's home if the vacancy had, in fact, been filled. The answer was no; the candidate had not started work. So at this point we reported to my regional office that the vacancy was still open and asked whether permission could be given for her to take the job.

KING: Who dealt with this in your office? Was it yourself or somebody working under you?

COOK: I was told about it in the first place, and I then asked the officer who is in charge of my women's section to deal with it. She found out the facts and interviewed Miss Ginetio herself.

KING: Would it have been dealt with at such a high level if the original inquiry hadn't come from an M.P.?

COOK: Yes, it would because the officer concerned is one of the comparatively few in the office who would be thoroughly familiar with the regulations in such cases and she would need, if not to do the interview herself, certainly to oversee the whole affair.

KING: As Mr Cook says, he found that, although by now several weeks had gone by, the position at the Warwick House Short Stay Unit that Flora had originally been offered, was still vacant. Somebody else had accepted it but then not turned up for work. The matron was getting pretty desperate. So Bob Cook reported the situation to his superior, who concluded that, after all, even though the Warwick House job wasn't a living-in job, Flora should be allowed to take it. First she couldn't have it; now she could. I put it to Bill Winter that he or somebody had a certain amount of discretion.

WINTER: We had, I think, discretion in recommendation, in the sense that the matron of the home had had considerable difficulty in filling this job, and the system anyway is flexible, you know, in the sense that, if we cannot find people to fill the job, then it is possible for a girl from abroad to take the job. So it's a question really of the flexibility of the regulations and flexibility, if I may say so, is admirably illustrated in this case.

KING: How many cases of this general sort come up?

WINTER: Oh, it's very difficult to give any kind of number to this. I think I can say that we do deal with considerable numbers of these cases throughout the year in the Midlands Region.

KING: Who took the final decision? Was the decision taken in Small Heath, in your office, or in London?

WINTER: The area of report, if I may call it that, was in the Small Heath Employment Exchange. The area of recommendation was in my office, the Regional Office, but the area of decision was in London. In other words, I made the recommendation from here in Birmingham. The decision was taken in London.

KING: You know the position here on the ground. Would you take it for granted that most of your recommendations, in this sort of case, would be accepted once they got to London?

WINTER: Generally, yes, I think my headquarters realise that we've a great deal of practical people in the regions, who know what they're talking about, and their recommendations are looked at and listened to very seriously.

KING: The formal decisions in these matters are taken by senior civil servants and, ultimately, by ministers in Whitehall. But, as Flora's case makes clear, the permanent officials working with these problems day to day do have an enormous responsibility. I asked John Hamilton, when he sits in his office in Holborn, far away from somebody like Flora, how conscious is he that he is taking decisions that are actually going to have a very substantial effect on people's lives?

HAMILTON: I don't think that you can do any sort of case

work which involves people without automatically thinking about the background of the person and what the information you have on him or her reveals about their background and personality and indeed their present position and predicament. And I think it's true and honest to say that we regard all applicants to us as human beings and members of the public.

KING: Does this degree of responsibility ever worry you? Do you find yourself lying awake at night wondering whether you've done the right thing?

HAMILTON: Yes, indeed, because so often the balance of public interest and policy against the wishes of an individual may be very finely balanced. If it is as close as that, the interest may be something much more important and, of course, has to be decided at a much higher level than mine.

KING: So Flora Ginetio got the work she wanted, working with mentally handicapped children. And she got what she wanted even more: the right to stay and live in Britain. And another typical Home Office/Department of Employment case had been dealt with, to everybody's satisfaction. Flora is working at the moment at the Warwick House centre.

But there is one question you have probably been asking yourself. How lucky was Flora Ginetio? How lucky was she to have as forceful a backer as Mrs Whitehouse? How lucky was she that a Member of Parliament took up her case? I asked Bill Winter in the Midlands Regional Office what would have happened to Flora if she had been on her own in this country, if she had not had Mrs Whitehouse behind her.

WINTER: This is a very difficult question to decide. It is true that in her backer she had an articulate and intelligent champion who did the right thing in going to Mr Roy Hattersley, although, as I said earlier, she could in fact have come to us, and we should have put her on the right lines. But I think it would have been extremely difficult for Miss Ginetio, with her perhaps limited command of English and her limited knowledge of how government departments work, to make her way, on her own, after having had her original application rejected.

KING: But Mrs Whitehouse did go to her local M.P. How much difference did it make that Flora's cause was now being championed, not by an ordinary member of the public, but by a Member of Parliament? The civil servants we talked to were emphatic that it made very little difference, if any. Bill Winter in Birmingham.

WINTER: I don't know that it made a great deal of difference, except that it was very helpful that Mr Hattersley had written to me because I know him and he knows me. But, having said that, I think I ought to make it perfectly clear that, if the case had been brought to our notice through other channels, the result would have been exactly the same.

KING: Likewise John Hamilton in London.

HAMILTON: I think I can say with complete honesty that there would have been no different decision in this case, whether Mr Hattersley had taken it up or not, provided that a second approach had been made, and indeed it would not have been dealt with at my level; it would have been dealt with at a lower level in the Immigration and Nationality Department.

KING: Roy Hattersley, perhaps predictably, is not so sure.

HATTERSLEY: I accept a general view that very often constituents come to their Members of Parliament when they could do the job for themselves, in theory. In practice, of course, it's a great deal easier simply for a Member of Parliament to have a conversation with a bureaucrat than it is for the man in the street. But I think that, as far as this case is concerned, the proof of the pudding is really in Flora's continued presence here. The letter she got said she had to go home. The letter I obtained said she could stay. And I think it's difficult to argue, in the face of that, that a Member of Parliament's interceding didn't make some sort of alteration in the judgement.

KING: What it seems to come down to is this. M.P.s don't influence the content of decisions; they do not have pull or 'influence' in that sense. But they do know their way round Westminster and Whitehall better than the rest of us, and, at the very least, when a Member of Parliament intervenes, civil servants and ministers do pay attention. An M.P. may not get the outcome he wants, but, if he raises a problem, he can be sure that it will be taken pretty seriously. And most M.P.s seem to be convinced that they and their constituents can expect reasonable and fair treatment. I asked Roy Hattersley what he would have done next if the Department of Employment had said that Flora could not have the job she particularly wanted, and had also said that there was not another job for her.

HATTERSLEY: It never struck me that the Department of Employment would not find her another job. Had they not done so, I would have gone and seen them, and I would have argued with them pretty fiercely because of my strong views about the nature of the case. Had they continued to refuse, I would have raised it in the House because it would have been the result of a silly bureaucratic mistake, and the Minister would not try to support that kind of mistake. In fact, the fact that I call it a mistake does not imply that I thought the Department would do it; it implies that I was sure the Department would not make that sort of mistake and would find her a job.

KING: How much time does Roy Hattersley reckon he spent on the Flora Ginetio case?

HATTERSLEY: It's certainly hours rather than days. It's probably two or three hours. It's an hour in their presence talking to them on three Saturday mornings, twenty minutes each time, it's half a dozen letters written, it's four phone calls made, and it's a few minutes worrying. It's two or three hours.

KING: Taking all the time he spends on constituency work, how much time does it add up to over the average week?

HATTERSLEY: About two-thirds of my week is done on parliamentary work of one sort or another, most of which is now constituency work. I've got a constituency with a lot of individual problems and therefore I have an uncharacteristically high load of constituency cases, and certainly rather more than three days a week is spent in the constituency doing political things or dealing with individual cases concerning the constituency.

KING: Anthony Royle as a minister puts a lot of effort into answering the letters M.P.s write on behalf of constituents. We asked him whether, as a member of Her Majesty's Government, he ever gets impatient having to spend so much time on details of this kind.

ROYLE: Oh no, certainly not. I've been a Member of Parliament for twelve years, and one of the jobs of a Member of Parliament, as indeed one of the jobs of a minister, is to keep in touch with the public, and if the public have complaints and they come to a minister through a Member of Parliament, it is the duty of a minister, and a duty which I find interesting and valuable, to make certain that this member of the public receives as much satisfaction as it's possible to obtain.

KING: How much time does he have as a minister to deal with his own constituents' complaints?

ROYLE: Well, quite a lot. I get out to my constituency once a month for advisory sessions, in Richmond, and my constituents come to see me with their worries and I write in the normal way to other colleagues who are ministers taking up their complaints. After all, a minister would not be a minister if he wasn't elected there by his constituents and, naturally, as a minister one's constituency comes first in one's life. It must always do.

KING: Anthony Royle implies that, as a minister, he gets no more favourable treatment, as far as his constituency work is concerned, than any other Member of Parliament. Roy Hattersley was until June 1970 a minister himself. Now he is a private Member on the Opposition side. Does he feel that the cases he raises are taken less seriously on account of this?

HATTERSLEY: Not on this sort of case at all. Clearly, on policy matters which affect one's constituents one has less influence. But on these matters of individual interpretation I have no doubt at all that the civil service treat Opposition Members and members of the Government with equal fairness. Indeed, one of the great difficulties when I was a minister in the D.E.P. was dealing with civil servants who were determined to lean over backwards to give my constituents no greater favours than anybody else. I think there's an objectivity in the civil service and I think it's a very healthy thing.

KING: But in the end doesn't all this constituency work, doesn't the writing of all these letters, the holding of surgeries and advisory sessions, boil down to an effort to win votes, to make sure of getting in next time? Roy Hattersley, and I think most M.P.s would deny this vigorously. How much help, I asked Roy Hattersley, do you think your constituency work is going to help towards your re-election when the time comes?

HATTERSLEY: Very little indeed. My re-election when the time comes depends on the standing of the two parties. I hope I shall poll about nineteen or twenty thousand votes. If two or three hundred of those are the result of my constituency work, I shall have done rather well.

KING: Why, then, does he do the work?

HATTERSLEY: I do the constituency work, not for a political

bonus because there isn't a political bonus in it. I do it because it's part of the job.

KING: Part of an M.P.'s job. The non-partisan, non-speech-making, little-publicised part that goes on week in and week out, even when Parliament is in recess.

Oh yes, we almost forgot. Flora Ginetio is to be married in June – to a Birmingham boy she first met visiting the Whitehouse family when she was sixteen. So she'll probably be spending the rest of her life in Britain. Roy Hattersley has been invited to the wedding.

3 The Ombudsman and Captain Horsley

In 'The Case of Flora Ginetio' we described in some detail how an individual Member of Parliament handled a typical constituency case: how it came to him, the government departments he got in touch with, and how eventually he got what was for him and the people who'd come to him a satisfactory outcome. In that particular case the Member of Parliament was always confident he'd get the right answer in the end – and he did.

But what if he hadn't? What if, to his surprise, the departments involved had simply dug in their heels and refused to budge? Ten years ago, even five years ago, that would have been the end of it. The M.P. couldn't really have done anything more, except maybe write an angry letter to the local paper.

Since April 1967, however, there has been something else he could do. He can now, if he wants to, refer the case to the Parliamentary Commissioner for Administration – Britain's version of the Ombudsman. We are going to look in detail here at the office of the British Ombudsman – and at how he and his staff dealt with a fairly typical case that landed on their desks some months ago. As with Flora Ginetio, the final outcome in this case was a happy one, but, as we'll hear, the story began a very long time ago. Our hero – and hero seems the right word since he's a military man – is Captain R. C. Horsley, holder of the Military Cross and a retired regular army officer. Fully twenty years ago Captain Horsley, who is now seventy-eight and lives with his wife and a very large, friendly dog on the edge of Dartmoor, applied for a war pension. He suffered from a gastric ulcer which he believed to have been caused by his service during the First World War and aggravated during the Second. The Ministry of Pensions, as it then was, rejected Captain Horsley's application. 'Why?' we asked him.

Documentary broadcast on 1 January 1972.

HORSLEY: Chiefly, I think, because they thought that far too much was probably going to be spent on pensions generally. And they framed the regulations accordingly. So that people who went up to get a pension, with every prospect of getting one, to their amazement found that they were turned down. The very obvious cases – for instance, like losing an arm or a leg or something like that – the very obvious cases they often treated quite generously. But the borderline cases were certainly not treated well. Indeed, they were treated completely ruthlessly.

KING: And the department looked on you as a borderline case?

HORSLEY: Most definitely, in face of all the evidence. Not only the evidence in my medical record, but the evidence on me. So naturally I was very indignant about it, but I went on trying and just nothing happened.

KING: At first, there wasn't a great deal Captain Horsley could do, beyond putting his case to the Pensions Appeal Tribunal. This he did, but again his application was turned down. Then a long time later, in 1965, a decision in one of the courts had the effect of making it probable that, if he were to reapply, this time his application would be successful. But, of course, nobody told him about the court's decision. And it wasn't until another four years had passed, in 1969, that he finally heard about it, quite by chance from a friend. What happened next?

HORSLEY: Well, I went to the Officers' Association because, when I was nearly dead and given up, my wife nursed me back to health again, but the Officers' Association and the British Legion between them got things moving, you see, on my behalf – thanks to the efforts of these officers. And the War Office handed me what they call a compassionate pension for good service, but it wasn't a disability pension, you see. And I was entitled to one and I was jolly well going to get it if I could, and when I got better I went on fighting. And when I eventually got it, you see – much to my surprise, I may say – when I eventually got it, I said: 'Right, you see, you blighters have done me down for twenty years, I don't see why I shouldn't have my arrears.'

KING: And that was the nub of the matter. Captain Horsley had got his pension all right, but it was to be paid only from the day in 1969 when those acting for him first got in touch with the Department of Health and Social Security. It certainly wasn't backdated to 1951 when he'd first applied. It wasn't even going to be backdated to 1965, the date of the court decision that affected him even though he didn't know about it. Captain Horsley thought this was pretty monstrous. And it was at this point that the Officers' Association suggested he probably ought to get in touch with his M.P. Captain Horsley's M.P. is Peter Mills, the Conservative Member for the Torrington Division, which takes in that part of Dartmoor. I asked Mr Mills how Captain Horsley's predicament had first come to his notice.

MILLS: Well, he wrote to me, as many of my constituents do about their various problems. And I read his letter and immediately I was sympathetic to what he had to say and his problem. Now this isn't always so, but I was in this case.

KING: Being sympathetic, Peter Mills could have done a number of different things. He could have written to the relevant Minister, Sir Keith Joseph; he could have put down a Question in Parliament; he could, as I said before, have written angry letters to the papers. But in fact he did none of these things and instead referred the case straight away to the Parliamentary Commissioner for Administration, the Ombudsman. And he explained why.

MILLS: By his letter I could see that he'd tried every avenue there was. And, as I say, one almost develops a sort of second sense as to whether a thing is genuine or not, and I felt this ought to go straight to the Ombudsman – for him to decide, of course, whether it was in his range for him to be able to do something about it.

KING: So now the case was on the Ombudsman's desk. More than that, it had arrived on his desk via the only route it could have travelled: not directly from Captain Horsley, but from Captain Horsley through a Member of Parliament. In Britain, unlike a number of other countries, you can't write directly to the Ombudsman with your problem. You have first to approach a Member of Parliament – not necessarily your own M.P., any M.P. Indeed, apart from some people's dislike of foreign words, that's the main reason why the British Ombudsman isn't formally called the Ombudsman but the Parliamentary Commissioner for Administration: the emphasis is on the word 'Parliamentary'. Practically everybody calls him the Ombudsman all the same, as Peter Mills confirms.

MILLS: It's very strange: if you gave him his proper title

people wouldn't know him at all. But by this strange – what is it? – Swedish or Danish name, 'Ombudsman', he is known to a very large number of people. And all I can say is that, when people write in when they are dismayed, frustrated, angry at my decision, they say: 'Will you please put this to the Ombudsman?'

KING: The Ombudsman at the moment is Sir Alan Marre, a former senior civil servant, who was appointed to succeed the first holder of the office, Sir Edmund Compton, early in 1970. He and his staff of just under sixty people work on the first and second floors of Church House, a large ecclesiastical-looking office building just round the corner from Westminster Abbey. I put it to Sir Alan that, when a case is referred to him by an M.P., he first has to decide whether it falls within his jurisdiction.

MARRE: This is so. We have what we call a screening test in the office, testing the cases that come to us against various provisions in the Act which exclude things from jurisdiction.

KING: What broadly falls within your jurisdiction? What sorts of things can you handle?

MARRE: Broadly what falls within my jurisdiction are complaints against government departments.

KING: But not complaints against, say, the nationalised industries or local authorities?

MARRE: No. Nor complaints against hospital authorities either.

KING: So the British Ombudsman – again unlike the Ombudsman in some other countries – isn't permitted under the law to take up every case involving government that is brought to him. Local government is left out, so are the Regional Hospital Boards and so are the big public corporations – the National Coal Board and so on. All he can deal with are cases – and not even all of these – which concern departments of central government – Whitehall, in other words. As regards Whitehall, the Ombudsman's remit is to concern himself with cases of maladministration, or at least suspected maladministration. And what, you may well ask, is maladministration? I asked Sir Alan.

MARRE: The Act itself under which I operate contains no definition of maladministration. And Mr Crossman, who was then Leader of the House, and was piloting the Bill through the House, explained maladministration as best he could by what came to be known as 'the Crossman catalogue'.

KING: And what's in the catalogue?

MARRE: In the catalogue he listed as examples 'bias, neglect, inattention, delay, incompetence, ineptitude, perversity, turpitude, arbitrariness', and so on.

KING: I take it you are not concerned with the question of justice: provided an unjust decision was reached in a proper way, that's all you need to know about?

MARRE: This is exactly so. The Act itself precludes me from questioning what are called the merits of decisions which are reached without maladministration.

KING: In other words, if Sir Alan Marre is to investigate a case, he must have some reason to think, not just that a particular decision taken somewhere in government is a wrong decision or an unfair decision, he must suspect that the decision was not arrived at properly or is in some way clearly indefensible. In practice it's pretty well up to the Ombudsman to define maladministration as he goes along – by the kinds of cases he takes up and the kinds he leaves alone. Alan Marre described the procedure he follows when a case like Captain Horsley's comes up.

MARRE: When I receive a complaint through a Member of Parliament, my first step is to arrange to get advice within the office whether it is within jurisdiction. If I'm satisfied that it is within jurisdiction, I then refer the case to the department for their comments. When I receive their comments, I then refer it to the unit in my office which is concerned with the affairs of that department. And what then happens normally is that the unit will get hold of the files – sometimes they are very bulky files – from the department; they will interview officers of the department to supplement information on the file or information which has been received with the complaint; and they will also interview in many cases the complainant himself or other people.

KING: The man in the Ombudsman's office who got hold of Captain Horsley's bulky file – and, incidentally, I've seen the outside of it and it really is bulky, about four inches thick – was Peter Wickham, who works in the unit that deals with Health and Social Security cases. His first job, presumably, was to go through the file and get the general picture?

WICKHAM: That's right, yes. And then to compile a statement for reference to the Department of Health for their comments.

KING: And how did they reply?

WICKHAM: The initial complaint concerned backdating to 1951, and their reply satisfied us that there wasn't any justification for such backdating. But it did reveal that Captain Horsley's case had succeeded as a result of a change in the interpretation of Article 4 of the Royal Warrant.

KING: The Royal Warrant being the instrument under which service pensions are dealt with. Did Mr Wickham then feel that he should go down and see Captain Horsley?

WICKHAM: Yes. Prior to seeing Captain Horsley we also went to see a representative of the Officers' Association who were acting on behalf of Captain Horsley.

KING: What sort of questions did you put to him that you couldn't put to the Department?

WICKHAM: To Captain Horsley you mean?

KING: Yes.

WICKHAM: The main purpose of seeing Captain Horsley was to find out what had prompted him to raise his case in 1969 – eighteen years after his initial claim – and also to find out whether he was aware of the judgement which had affected his case and allowed it to succeed.

KING: So that this trip all the way down to Devon was actually pretty useful. It added to your stock of information.

WICKHAM: Oh indeed it did, yes.

KING: Captain Horsley was certainly happy to see Peter Wickham.

HORSLEY: They were most helpful. They sent down a member of their staff who, incidentally, treated me with a courtesy which was quite a change from the treatment I received on my return from Malaya, which was perfectly scandalous. I'm not the only one of course. The treatment I received on my return from Malaya was, as I say, perfectly shocking. And to have somebody from the Parliamentary Commissioner's office treating one as one expected one should be treated was, I may say, a delightful change. And he was very efficient and very helpful. And he went into matters very thoroughly.

KING: The procedure followed by the Ombudsman, as both Sir Alan Marre and Peter Wickham have said, involved the executive department concerned more or less from the beginning. It's up to the department to open its files to the Ombudsman and to explain to him the reasons for the decisions it's taken. David Ward is an Assistant Secretary, a senior official in the Department of Health and Social Security. Just how seriously cases coming from the Ombudsman are taken in the Department is indicated by his answer when I asked him how his own role in Captain Horsley's case changed when the Parliamentary Commissioner became involved.

WARD: When it became a Parliamentary Commissioner case, then it became one in which the Permanent Secretary was directly interested, so it was no longer possible – even if it had been desirable – for me to make a decision on my own accord in consultation with our lawyers as to what line we should take with Captain Horsley on the matter of the payment of arrears. Once it became a Parliamentary Commissioner case, the case simply had to go through my hands, once I'd looked at it from a policy point of view, to the Under-Secretary and then right up to the top, to the Permanent Secretary.

KING: So at this point it became a question for the top leadership in the Department.

WARD: Yes, it became one for top-level administration.

KING: The Under-Secretary in charge of war pensions in the Department, a more senior official, is Robert Windsor. We talked generally about the attitude a department like his takes when the Ombudsman begins to show an interest in something. 'What is your reaction when the Ombudsman does take a case up? Do you feel that suddenly this is a matter that assumes particular importance, that you have to handle particularly carefully?'

WINDSOR: Well, yes and no to that question. Quite clearly, a case taken up by the Parliamentary Commissioner does require considerable attention. After all, we are seeking equity here, and here we have a case where a complainant genuinely feels we've been inequitable. In that sense it has to have particular attention. But if you mean that everyone gets to panic-stations, including me, well my answer is no, they don't.

KING: Does it worry you at all to have somebody from the Parliamentary Commissioner's office coming round here and talking to your subordinates and rooting around in the files and so on?

WINDSOR: No, it doesn't worry me in the slightest, because – if I may say so, Professor – we can give as good as we get; but we accept that the Parliamentary Commissioner and his staff have a job to do. In fact their objective is the same as ours; they are trying to ensure that fair and reasonable dealings – no, not dealings – decisions are made with regard to every person who has a claim. So the basic objective is identical, even if we come at it from a rather different angle.

KING: So several weeks after he'd first heard from Peter Mills, Sir Alan Marre had in front of him a complete dossier on the case, with Peter Wickham's factual report on the top of the pile. From then on it was a matter for him to deal with personally.

MARRE: Having examined the papers, the conclusion that I reached was that Captain Horsley's original complaint – that is, that his award of pension had not been backdated to 1951 – could not, in my view, reasonably be upheld, but that there was another possibility of a more limited backdating which the Department had not conceded, and which it seemed to me ought to be further considered. And at this stage I wrote to the Department inviting them to consider this other alternative. After they had considered this, the Department still felt their original decision was right, and wrote back and said so. But I still felt that perhaps the arguments for the alternative backdating hadn't been fully considered, and so I wrote again to the Department, and I suggested that perhaps a meeting between me and the head of that side of the Department might be useful. And we did have a meeting. The Department reviewed the facts again at the end of the day and, I'm glad to say, changed their minds.

KING: The other possibility, the alternative backdating Sir Alan referred to, was the idea of paying Captain Horsley his pension, not indeed all the way back to 1951, but to 1965, when the decision by the courts affecting Captain Horsley and others like him, was originally handed down. This seems on the face of it a fair and sensible solution. I put it to Robert Windsor why, in the light of this, the Department had been so reluctant to change its mind.

WINDSOR: Well, the decision we made was within the framework of a rule which we believed to be reasonable and equitable, and which for good measure two Parliamentary Commissioners had agreed was reasonable and equitable. If you're going to break these rules, the awful problem is: what's the good of curing one anomaly if you make two as a result? But nevertheless in the event we did decide that this rule might be capable of some refinement, or development, and it was in that sense that we accepted in the event the Parliamentary Commissioner's quite strongly held view.

KING: So in the end the Department did alter its rule. But let's suppose the Department had, even despite the strongly held views of the Ombudsman, simply dug in its heels. What could Sir Alan Marre have done about it? The short answer is 'almost nothing'. The Parliamentary Commissioner doesn't have the power to issue orders or instructions to government departments, or even to take them to court. The most he can do, as his name implies, is simply to report to Parliament – in other words, to make the whole thing public. I asked Sir Alan: 'Of the three hundred or so cases you deal with every year, how many are settled to your satisfaction?'

MARRE: The great majority are settled to my satisfaction.

KING: Has there ever been a clear-cut case where you have hoped, wished, recommended, invited the department to change its view, and it simply and flatly at the end of the day said 'No'?

MARRE: There have been one or two cases, but these are fairly my office, and it's similar to what goes on in other countries with similar offices. All I can do is to make a report to a government exceptional. But that is quite clearly part of the whole set-up of department, leaving it to the government department, if they are persuaded, to put matters that I feel have gone wrong, right. If they disagree with my view at the end of the day, theirs is the decision, but the Member of Parliament will know, Parliament itself will know, and if they think it proper to take the matter further it can be further pursued in Parliament.

KING: But in Captain Horsley's case the Department didn't in the end disagree with Sir Alan's view. His pension wasn't backdated as far as he thought it should have been, but it was backdated. Is he grateful to the Ombudsman?

HORSLEY: Grateful I most certainly am. As I say, he can't work miracles, but he got me £400 where nobody else could anyway, and that's something for a retired captain, believe me.

KING: And he isn't the only one who's convinced that, but for the Ombudsman, his case would never have been reopened, let alone a different decision come to. The Member of Parliament's answer was as categorical as it was brief. 'Do you think, in fact, there was ever a serious chance that he would have got his pension backdated unless the Ombudsman had intervened?'

MILLS: No.

KING: And Robert Windsor of the Department conceded the

Westminster and Beyond *by King and Sloman*

CORRIGENDUM

On p. 36 the fourth paragraph should begin:

MARRE: There have been one or two cases, but these are fairly exceptional. But that is quite clearly part of the whole set-up of my office, and it's similar to what goes on in other countries with similar offices. All I can do is to make a report to a government point equally readily. The Parliamentary Commissioner had been decisive.

WINDSOR: He was decisive in the event that he brought a different eye, a different angle to bear, and in the event after much consideration this was an angle which we accepted was leading to greater equity and fairness, and so we certainly have to attribute that to the Parliamentary Commissioner.

KING: If the Ombudsman can take up a case like Captain Horsley's, can get a department to look at it again, and can often in the end get a better, fairer decision, certain obvious questions arise. Shouldn't the Ombudsman's jurisdiction be expanded to cover, say, local government and the nationalised industries? Shouldn't he be given more power? Shouldn't the ordinary citizen be able to get in touch with him directly, instead of having to work through an M.P.? Because it does seem at first glance that, given the Ombudsman's potential, the scope of his office at the moment is terribly restricted. Does Sir Alan Marre himself think complaints should continue to reach him only via the Member of Parliament?

MARRE: I think that it is part of the whole constitutional set-up under which we operate in this country. We are the largest country in terms of population to have an office of this kind and, if there weren't some screen like the M.P., if there was direct access by an aggrieved member of the public to me, I think the volume of stuff that I would get would be far greater than a single person could cope with, and certainly beyond my capacity to deal with personally.

KING: At the moment you have only the power to recommend and report, and make a case public. Do you think you should have more power? Do you think you should have the power ever to decide?

MARRE: No, I don't myself think this would be right. I said earlier that in other countries the corresponding holders of similar posts do not have this power, and I think at the end, in the end of the day that is, decisions must ultimately rest with the Government.

KING: When the office of Parliamentary Commissioner was first set up a little under five years ago, a lot of M.P.s were worried that this new dignitary would in some way detract from their position: the Member of Parliament after all was the person to whom people in Britain had traditionally taken their grievances. This antagonism towards the Ombudsman hasn't entirely died away even now. I asked Peter Mills whether he felt his position had been in any way diminished by the Ombudsman, or whether it had been strengthened.

MILLS: No. I've always thought that I am a junior Ombudsman. I've always felt that we stand between constituents and the executive. So I have no feeling of jealousy at all. There comes a time when you get stuck, when you can't go any further with a case and indeed when your constituents have tried every avenue and can't get any further against the executive, and then it is right to have this Ombudsman, for him to look at it, and see what he can do.

KING: One of the obvious points about the Ombudsman as he exists in Britain is that he can deal only with the relationships between the public and central government, and indeed not all aspects of even central government. Do you think there's a case to be made out for widening his scope of authority?

MILLS: Yes, I do – now that it has been proved, to my mind at least, that it is a successful operation, and that he does a good job. And I think most M.P.s would agree on this. I believe it's right that it should be extended. And of course my own personal feeling is that it should be extended to the local government sector, where of course there are far more problems and difficulties than there are with ministries in London.

KING: How important does Mr Mills think it is, that the Ombudsman is independent of the Government of the day, and is seen to be independent?

MILLS: I think it's terribly important, that's why I'm very pleased that there is an Ombudsman, because, you see, so many constituents feel disillusioned, dismayed and angry at decisions made by ministers and ministries. They don't understand the language sometimes, and I believe it's terribly important that they can see that somebody stands back and has a sort of independent look. I believe they're prepared to accept that, because they don't look upon an Ombudsman as part of the Government, and they don't look on their M.P. as necessarily siding with the minister and his decision. And I think this is a very good thing for democracy.

KING: And in this case we really do have to come back to the individual, the ordinary citizen – or rather, *an* individual, *an* ordinary citizen – because if a satisfactory outcome couldn't have been reached without the Ombudsman it couldn't have been reached without Captain Horsley either. It was his indignation and his persistence over a period of twenty years that kept the whole issue alive. And as it happens Captain Horsley's success benefited a considerable number of other war pensioners who were in a similar situation. When I talked to him, Captain Horsley admited that, before he'd been in touch with the Officers' Association and his Member of Parliament, he'd only heard of the Parliamentary Commissioner in a pretty vague sort of way. I asked him whether he thought the office of the Ombudsman gets enough publicity.

HORSLEY: I think his office should get a great deal more publicity. And what is more, he should be given a great deal more power, because he exercises it on behalf of the individual; he's the only resort we have now because the Monarchy is constitutional now and can no longer function in that way. I only hope he won't be overworked because he is the one parliamentary figure who is on the side of the individual as far as I can see. The ministries are out for their own yard-arm, and they don't give two damns for anybody else except themselves.

KING: A little sweeping maybe, but then Captain Horsley did have a grievance.

4 Selecting Candidates: The Secret Garden

It used to be called the 'secret garden of British politics', and a few years ago an American commentator claimed that the garden remained secret partly because our political parties deliberately kept the gates locked – and even patrolled the walls to keep outsiders from peering over. What was in the garden was the way the parties went about selecting their parliamentary candidates. *Elections*, yes, they were public, and everybody knew about them. But *selections* – oh no – they were a private matter to be decided by the political parties internally, by themselves, away from the public gaze.

Well, the parties are a lot less secretive than they used to be, but candidate selection is still an aspect of politics most people don't know much about – despite the fact that, in safe seats, to be selected by the party that holds the seat is tantamount to being elected, and despite the fact that, even in marginal seats, voters don't have a free choice among all possible candidates but have to make do with the candidates the parties chose to present them with. How do the parties go about selecting the people they want you and me to vote for? Who takes part? What qualities are the selectors looking for? How much say do the parties' headquarters in London have?

The best way of answering these questions we thought was to explore in detail a couple of recent selections – typical ones preferably, but, if they turned out to have an odd feature or two, so much the better. And we lit on two constituencies where there have recently been by-elections: at Arundel and Shoreham, one of the safest Tory seats in the country, and Southampton, Itchen, an almost equally impregnable seat on the Labour side. Let Richard Luce, one of the Conservative contenders at Arundel

---

Documentary broadcast on 5 June 1971.

and Shoreham, describe what happened after he read in the papers one day last December that, because of the death of the sitting M.P., Arundel and Shoreham was vacant. He'd already fought another seat at the general election.

LUCE: When I heard there was a vacancy, I wrote to the Vice-Chairman of the Party, knowing, of course, that my name was already on the list, since I had fought in the election before, and asked that my name should go forward for consideration for Arundel and Shoreham.

KING: Had you, in fact, ever been there before?

LUCE: I had never been in the area at all, no.

KING: Presumably a letter arrived more or less out of the blue one day from the people of Arundel and Shoreham inviting you to come and see them?

LUCE: Yes, a telephone call came and invited me for a first interview.

KING: And that was to see the Selection Committee?

LUCE: That was to see the Selection Committee, yes.

KING: A relatively small group of people.

LUCE: A group of I think between twenty and twenty-five.

KING: And what happened that day?

LUCE: Well, like many others – I think there were eighteen or nineteen of us – I was invited for about thirty-five to forty minutes, to go before the Committee, to make a very brief speech, I think three or four minutes, about why I wanted to be a Member of Parliament. And then I answered questions for about half an hour.

KING: Richard Luce's name had been sent along to the Arundel and Shoreham Association by the Vice-Chairman of the Conservative Party responsible for candidates, an M.P. himself, called William Elliott, The Vice-Chairman keeps the central list of approved candidates that Richard Luce referred to. 'How,' I asked William Elliott, 'does someone go about getting on to it?'

ELLIOTT: The short answer to that is that he writes to me as the Vice-Chairman of the Party, and he receives from me a form which he fills in. This requires him to give certain particulars about himself, and requires him also to name sponsors to whom we can write asking about him. The longer answer, of course, is that before he gets to the stage of writing to ask me for a form he should become known to the Conservative Party in the area in which he lives.

KING: And you take up references from the sponsors, rather as though he were an applicant for a job?

ELLIOTT: I think this is necessary, you know. We need to know, before we start on the procedure of interviewing and so on, that the person concerned is a sound, decent person, who has some knowledge of politics and public life, and who is, above all else, a good Conservative.

KING: You refer to the procedure of interviewing. How are the interviews conducted, and by whom?

ELLIOTT: Well, initially, once the candidate, or prospective candidate, has filled in his form and sent it up to our office here, he comes to see me. And, depending on whether I think he is worthy of being taken on further, he will eventually see two members of an Advisory Panel which helps me in these matters, composed mainly, but not entirely, of Members of Parliament.

KING: Not everyone's name is added to the approved list, but Richard Luce's was. And, when he was asked to be considered at Arundel and Shoreham, Conservative Central Office in London automatically forwarded his biographical details to the local Association. But he wasn't the only would-be Tory M.P. interested. On the contrary, Arundel and Shoreham is a peculiarly attractive seat – quite apart from the huge Conservative majority, it's in lovely country on the Sussex coast, within easy travelling distance of London – and applications came pouring in. I asked Noel Barker, the Chairman of the constituency Association, how many there were in the end.

BARKER: Well, in all we had 173 applications. Some of them came direct to us.

KING: And how did you sift them out? How did you get down from 173 to three?

BARKER: Well, we had a Selection Committee which was formed of the Finance and General Purposes Committee of the Association, and we went through the biographical details of every one of those 173 people in detail. We read them, we then signed that we'd read them, and we also signed in another column to say whether or not we wished to interview them.

KING: And you got the list down to . . .?

BARKER: . . . In the end to nineteen.

KING: And, after all nineteen had been interviewed, the Selection Committee reduced the number to three: someone who'd once been political secretary to Edward Heath; a young financial analyst who used to work for the party's Research Department; and Richard Luce, who at the age of thirty-four had already been a civil servant in Kenya, and who was Director of the National Suggestions Centre. So far everything had proceeded along fairly orthodox lines; but the next thing the Selection Committee did was rather unusual. It decided that the final selection with about a hundred people present should take place, not in a hired hall somewhere, but after a buffet luncheon at a seaside hotel. Richard Luce remembers it well.

LUCE: It was an extremely enjoyable lunch. I can remember the chicken very well, and the rice, and it was very informal. Of course, being one of the short-listed candidates, we were very tensed up, but it was informal and relaxing, and one went round and talked to people in a very relaxed manner, I thought, and they were very friendly to us.

KING: And then you made a short speech to this larger group?

LUCE: And then I made a longer speech – I think it was ten to fifteen minutes – to the larger group, yes.

KING: Standing up there in front of the members of the Executive Council, what did Richard Luce think they were looking for in their new M.P.?

LUCE: Do you know I really honestly don't know. And I'm not sure that I even know now. I think that's really for the Chairman of the Association to say.

KING: The Chairman of the Association did have pretty clear ideas.

BARKER: We had three principal things I think that we were looking for. Firstly, someone in an age group which was not too old. Secondly, we wanted a very good constituency Member, because many of our constituents are old people; they need looking after. And, thirdly, we wanted a man who we thought would go a long way in politics – in other words, a high-flyer.

KING: And in the end, after two ballots with first one of the three contenders being eliminated and then the other, the Executive Council of the Arundel and Shoreham Conservative Association decided that they had found their high-flyer in Richard

Luce. But there was another rather peculiar feature of this particular selection: the presence outside the hotel where the luncheon was taking place of several Women's Liberation demonstrators. They were there, not because there were no women on the short-list, but because the men's wives had also been invited to the lunch. Had there, I asked Noel Barker, been any discussion about whether or not the wives should be summoned in this way?

BARKER: I don't think there was any discussion. We had never thought of doing otherwise.

KING: You assumed that this was the natural thing to do. Why?

BARKER: Yes. Well, I can only give you my personal opinion here, though I think it is shared by members of my Association. We think that the wife of a Member is immensely important. We hold many social events throughout the year, and throughout our branches, and we like the Member's wife to attend them and get to know people, and they get to know her, and it's very popular. And it was nice to just see the wives, I think. I don't say that they would have made any difference to the final choice, but it was nice to see them anyway.

KING: What about Mrs Luce, Richard's wife? Was she surprised at all when the invitation came?

MRS LUCE: No, I wasn't, because exactly the same had happened when he was selected for Hitchin four years before. I was asked to go along to the meeting.

KING: And what happened at the lunch?

MRS LUCE: It was a very informal, very friendly affair. We just had a good lunch and walked round talking to people.

KING: Were you asked any formal questions before the whole assemblage of people?

MRS LUCE: Yes, but purely personal ones – what were my hobbies, and whether I'd be prepared to go to women's meetings.

KING: Do you thing it's right that wives should be looked at in this way?

MRS LUCE: I think it's fair enough they should go along, but I'd be very against them making any political comments or speeches at all.

KING: Mrs Luce has actually had a lot of political experience herself. Her father was an M.P. and she's been secretary to two other M.P.s. Did it ever occur to her that she might get selected herself instead of her husband?

MRS LUCE: I'd have applied for the Chiltern Hundreds on the spot.

KING: So in the Tory Party it's the most natural thing in the world for wives to be vetted. Not so on the Labour side, where there's a mild air of outrage at the very idea. Why? I asked the Labour Party's National Agent, Ron Hayward.

HAYWARD: We claim to be of average intelligence in the Labour Party, you see, and the British electoral law says that the name of the candidate only shall be on the ballot paper. A Member's wife can play a very important part by her husband's side: she plays no part really in his parliamentary life; she plays her part at constituency level. So we would be very much against judging a man on his wife. One must be careful what we say on that, but there'll be plenty of husbands who would not want to be judged on their wives. I suppose vice versa would be the case too.

KING: As far as Mrs Luce's husband was concerned, there remained only the formality of the actual election. It came not long afterwards when he was returned as Conservative Member for Arundel with a majority of no less than 23,000. Given the constituency's Conservatism, the real choice of the Member of Parliament had already taken place.

And the situation wasn't so very different a few weeks later in the Itchen Division of Southampton. Itchen isn't quite as safe for Labour as Arundel and Shoreham is for the Conservatives, but it has been a Labour seat ever since it was created back in 1950. For fifteen years it was held by Dr Horace King. It was Dr King's retirement, both as M.P. for Itchen and as Speaker of the House of Commons, that led to the by-election. The Labour activists in Itchen selecting the new Labour candidate could be pretty sure that they were also choosing the new M.P.

As it happens, the Labour selection procedures are a bit more complicated than the Conservatives', and we asked Ron Hayward to explain them. If somebody wants to become a Labour M.P. how should he go about it?

HAYWARD: Well, he can do it in two ways. Either he can ask his Constituency Labour Party to nominate him on to their List B of possible parliamentary Labour candidates, or when he knows there is a selection conference pending he can write to the constituency party concerned and ask if he can be considered.

KING: Mention of a B List implies the existence of an A List. It sounds rather complicated.

HAYWARD: There's no mystery about it. The A List is a list of sponsored trade union candidates, which has been approved by the trade unions, and the B List is a list of possible candidates who have been nominated by constituency Labour parties. It's not an approved list; it's simply a list of names put forward by the constituency parties themselves.

KING: And you send these lists out automatically when a selection is taking place?

HAYWARD: Yes, both Lists A and B go automatically to the parties when they start their selection machinery.

KING: But one doesn't actually have to be on either to be selected?

HAYWARD: Indeed not, no, and often you find that parties will select people who are not on these lists. This is simply to give them a list of names so that they can invite people down to speak to them, to answer questions, before they start the actual selection machinery. But any member of the Labour Party can be nominated as a prospective parliamentary candidate.

KING: But, although you don't have to be on either of the two national lists, you do, if you want to be adopted as a Labour candidate, have to be nominated for selection locally – either by a ward party, or by an affiliated organisation: a trade union branch, say, or a women's section. You can't simply write in, in other words: you have to be able to produce some evidence of local backing. But in the case of one of the contenders at Itchen, Bob Mitchell, proving that he had local backing wasn't at all difficult, because until he was defeated at the general election in 1970 he was M.P. for the Test Division of Southampton right next door. He'd known in advance that Dr King was going to retire. What steps did he take to make sure he was taken seriously at Itchen?

MITCHELL: I didn't have to take any steps, because, I mean, obviously having represented Southampton Test, I knew I would be considered.

KING: Did you set out to get a large number of nominations? Did you go around the wards?

MITCHELL: I kept right out of the way during the whole course of the proceedings.

KING: Bob Mitchell was only one of several ex-Labour M.P.s defeated at the general election and looking for a new seat. Another was Christopher Price, former Member for Perry Barr in Birmingham. When he heard that Dr King was about to retire, what did he do?

PRICE: I was in something of a dilemma. I had known Bob Mitchell a very long time, I knew how he'd very much had to look after Dr King's seat while he was Speaker, politically, in a number of ways. On the other hand, I had spent a number of years as ward secretary in one of the wards in the Itchen constituency. I'd been on the executive, I'd been a delegate to conference from Itchen. What I did – well, I happened to be in Southampton on completely other business, visiting the university, and I dropped in on the chairman of the women's section of the ward party which I used to be secretary of. This was actually before Dr King had formally announced his retirement. And we chatted and it emerged that if he did actually retire I would quite like my name to go forward.

KING: Mrs Jean Harder is a subscription collector in another ward in the Division. How did her ward party go about deciding whom, if anybody, it was going to nominate?

HARDER: Well, it was discussed in the ward with the ward members, and it was a majority vote.

KING: When you say in the ward with ordinary members, was this in somebody's sitting-room, or a hall somewhere?

HARDER: Oh yes . . . it was in our sitting-room, yes.

KING: Did you seriously consider other candidates?

HARDER: Well, there were some that considered other candidates. There was another candidate nominated. But they said that they would abide by the majority rule.

KING: The job of looking at all the possible candidates and deciding on a short-list, the job that was done at Arundel and Shoreham by Noel Barker and the Association's Finance and General Purposes Committee, is always done on the Labour side by the local party's Executive Committee, with the larger General Management Committee having the final say. The short-list at Itchen was twice as long as at Arundel: six names, no less than four of them ex-M.P.s. The selection conference (about sixty people were there) was held shortly afterwards. Let Christopher Price tell it as he saw it.

PRICE: The selection conference took place on a Sunday afternoon. Actually we were frightfully late. I thought of Southampton as being seventy-odd miles from London and left a couple of hours to drive down in. It wasn't nearly enough: we exceeded every speed limit on the way down on the last bit. But we arrived virtually as the selection conference was about to start. And the press were all there and we walked into this hotel. I was surprised at this because my memory of Southampton Labour Party had been of the old party premises where I imagined the selection would take place. But they decided to do it rather grandly this time and they took a hotel.

They then, very officiously, segregated the candidates from the delegates and indeed the candidates from the candidates' wives. My wife was left sitting in a hotel armchair and drank tea all afternoon and read the Sunday papers. The six candidates were then put in a room by ourselves – some of us knew each other; there were two other former Members of Parliament, John Dunwoody and John Ellis. And we sort of talked pleasantries in one of these idiotic situations where you say 'Well, what have you been doing?' and this sort of thing. And you know that you are not talking about what you are actually thinking about. And then the tension builds up and some of us went out and walked on the common outside, and some of us stood around, and those who smoked smoked rather more than usual. And then I invited my wife to come and talk to us, since I didn't see there was any real point in her sitting all by herself. And this sort of loosened things up a bit. But the tension was very great when one walked into the room. Then it was all over terribly quickly. Ten minutes' talk and ten minutes' questions is absolutely no time at all when you come to think of it.

KING: And after the examination was all over, how long did you have to wait for the verdict?

PRICE: About fifteen minutes. It might have been a great deal longer, but in fact it was all settled on the first ballot. So the tension was not so bad. We really knew it was all over before they came in and told us, because there was a burst of applause from the delegates nearby. And although we discussed what it might be, I knew the only thing it could be was that Bob had won it on the first ballot.

KING: And then you drove home again.

PRICE: Well no, it was a little more awkward after that. Then we went in and sat there while they announced the result and we all congratulated Bob, and John Ellis – who was really his best friend in Parliament – another of the people on the short-list – made a very touching speech about how much Bob deserved it. And then the delegates dispersed, but the candidates had been invited to tea in this hotel with the president of the party. And so we sat there drinking tea and eating lettuce sandwiches at sort of six o'clock on a Sunday afternoon. And we chatted a bit and then jumped in the car and drove home, feeling a little empty.

KING: So Bob Mitchell it was. And soon afterwards, the Labour selection conference having done its work, the voters of Itchen did theirs and elected him to Parliament. Mrs Harder's ward had nominated Bob Mitchell. I asked her whether she'd been mandated to vote for him at the selection conference?

HARDER: No, no. It was an individual vote at the selection conference.

KING: What were you looking for in particular? Were you interested in somebody's political views, or his personality, or whether he had local connections, or what?

HARDER: I would say really my own personal view is he was a constituency man. We'd seen what he'd done and we judged him on his results.

KING: Why does Bob Mitchell think he'd won? Was it mainly his local connections?

MITCHELL: I think very largely. You know, I've lived in Southampton all my life, and when I was the Member of Parliament for Test I was in fact acting as the spokesman on the floor of the House of Commons for Itchen as well as Test – I mean because of Horace King's constitutional position. I think the delegates knew this and appreciated it.

KING: Bob Mitchell was selected at Southampton because he'd been a good constituency member, and at Arundel and Shoreham they also wanted a good constituency M.P. But what about *politics*? – not only the divisions between the two main parties, but the divisions inside them: the left/right controversy in the Labour Party, the divisions over Europe on the Conservative side,

If these two constituencies are typical, and in general they probably are, it seems these sorts of issues play some part but not very much. Selectors in most constituencies seem more interested in the quality of the men than in the details of their political views. William Elliott, the Conservative Vice-Chairman, is clearly looking mainly for personal qualities in someone he interviews.

ELLIOTT: First of all we want him to be a person of sound character – a genuine type who has thus far led a thoroughly respectable life, who understands basically what public life is all about, and who is public-life-minded as well as politically-minded.

KING: And Christopher Price was quite clear that there were no right- or left-wing factions at Itchen trying to put their candidates over.

PRICE: No. I mean you do in some constituencies, but in that constituency – which I knew well and knew to be very free of political factions within the party – I didn't get that sense at all.

KING: Of course we've been talking as though parliamentary candidates really are selected locally and not by the party bosses in London. But what reason is there to think that Richard Luce wasn't *really* the nominee of Central Office, and that Bob Mitchell wasn't *really* the man Transport House wanted to see chosen? The main answer is that local associations are proud of their right to select their parliamentary candidate, and would, if they had to, fight fiercely to defend it. I asked Noel Barker what would have been the reaction in Arundel and Shoreham if they'd got the feeling that Central Office was trying to push a particular person?

BARKER: I think it would have aroused great opposition in the constituency. It certainly would have aroused opposition in myself. Because we like to think that we can decide our own problems, and certainly one of this nature.

KING: Likewise I put it to Ron Hayward whether he, as Labour's National Agent, could have any influence on who a local party selected.

HAYWARD: None whatsoever. Although the National Executive Committee in parliamentary by-elections, but not in general elections, has the right to request a party to look at a particular individual, that's all they can do. And they very infrequently do that. So we can't really have any influence. The selection is made by accredited delegates to the General Management Committee and it's done on a secret ballot, so you couldn't possibly have any influence over it whatsoever.

KING: In this respect, then, the two parties are very similar. There is, though, one major difference between them – apart from the business of wives. In the Labour Party, trade unions can sponsor candidates. In other words, they can say, in effect, to a constituency party: 'If you select this member of our union, we'll make a substantial contribution to constituency funds and to our candidate's election expenses.' List A, referred to by Ron Hayward earlier, is a list of precisely such candidates. But, even within the Labour Party, a lot of people are critical of the whole role of trade unions in this field. I suggested to Ron Hayward that, in a constituency where the unions are strong, there's always a danger that the man selected will be not the best man but the man who is in the good books of the local union branches.

HAYWARD: I've often heard this said, you know, but if I could state a personal preference I would very, very much like to see more trade union candidates selected. And I want to see the strongest possible contingent of trade union candidates in the Commons. This is not always so. And in the case of Southampton it has a tradition that it does not select sponsored candidates. This party believes it should find the money itself and it does so.

KING: What about on the Conservative side? If I'm a wealthy Tory, can I buy myself a nomination by offering to contribute handsomely to party funds? William Elliott:

ELLIOTT: Not any more. No, no. Not since the Maxwell-Fyfe Committee reported twenty-odd years ago. According to the rules of the Conservative Party, a sum, a small sum, of money is the fixed sum which any candidate can subscribe to his election funds. So that we have as a party eliminated altogether the possibility of money playing any sort of part at all. It's ability and general soundness of character which count – not money.

KING: Money clearly isn't the issue it used to be. But there is one other question that worries a lot of people, outside politics as well as in. At Arundel and Shoreham, a safe Conservative seat, Richard Luce was chosen as Member of Parliament by no more than about a hundred people – perhaps a hundred and fifty. Similarly, at Southampton only about sixty people attended the selection conference that chose Bob Mitchell, and probably no more than another hundred or so were involved in the making of nominations beforehand. Is it right, especially in safe seats, that such a big decision should rest in the hands of so few people? I put this question to almost everybody we talked to. The answers were interesting. According to Noel Barker, the proof of the pudding is in the eating.

BARKER: We have arrived at the result which has met with the approval of the whole constituency, and I can say that without any thought of any opposition, because Richard Luce has now been round to every one of our branches, and as I travel round I get only praise. So it shows that our system must have worked pretty well, I think.

KING: William Elliott maintained that in reality more people were involved in candidate selection than seemed to be. 'Isn't there a case,' I asked him, 'for broadening the basis of selection to include, say, ordinary rank-and-file party workers, or possibly even ordinary voters for the party?'

ELLIOTT: But then they *are* included, and this I would wish to stress. The local Conservative association is invariably representative of all sections of the community and of senior members of the association, junior members of the association, our women's organisation and so on. So that I would really like to emphasise to you that the average selection committee is, I believe, wholly representative of the community, of the Conservative community of course, the active Conservative community of the association concerned.

KING: Ron Hayward is just as satisfied with his party's procedures. Like William Elliott, he maintains that, even if ordinary party workers aren't actively involved in selecting candidates, they are represented.

HAYWARD: Well, it is true, of course, that a small number of people, as you say, made the selection of Bob Mitchell. But these people were accredited delegates who were appointed by an affiliated organisation to the Southampton Labour Party, and represented their point of view. So I don't think really that we should worry about that. This is a democratic procedure which we've carried out for nearly forty years. And it works. Now if you mean would I like to see more people involved? Yes, I would.

KING: But perhaps the simple truth of the matter for both parties was best expressed by an ordinary Labour Party worker,

Mrs Harder. When she was out collecting subscriptions last winter, did people ever refer to the fact that Horace King was about to retire?

HARDER: Oh yes, they said who was going to take Horace King's place, you know. They said we'd have to select somebody else now.

KING: Did anybody ever express any views as to who his successor ought to be?

HARDER: Well no, although they are members of the Labour Party, they don't come to ward meetings and they really only get involved at election time. You know, the time between doesn't really . . .

KING: So it was really left up to a rather small number of people to do the actual selecting?

HARDER: As in everything – yes.

KING: So the secret garden of British politics has yielded up its secrets – most of them anyway. Cumbersome procedures, certainly; not very democratic procedures, possibly. But the two parties' procedures do seem to work and, after all, if we don't like the results, all we have to do is vote against the candidates the parties select, or maybe even run for Parliament ourselves.

5 Women in Parliament

'Sir,' said Samuel Johnson in the middle of the eighteenth century, 'a woman's preaching is like a dog's walking on his hinder legs. It is not done well, but you are surprised to find it done at all.' And that, even in the middle of the twentieth century, is still the view sometimes held about women as politicians. Women don't make good politicians, it's said, and even if they did they don't really belong in politics. Now we're not going to spend time disputing this view, we're simply going to ignore it. It seems to us too obvious to be worth arguing about that women are in politics, to stay, that many of them are very good at it, and that a woman's place is just as much in politics as in any other occupation requiring qualities, ideally, of intelligence, honesty and courage.

Instead of defending the role of women in politics, we've tried, with the help of the BBC Sound Archives and several women now in the House of Commons, to find out what it feels like to be a woman politician, what handicaps they think they labour under, if any, how much fellow-feeling there is amongst women in different parties, and so on. Our interviews are with Barbara Castle, Dame Patricia Hornsby-Smith, Margaret Thatcher, and Shirley Williams. From the past we'll be hearing the views of Lady Astor, Eleanor Rathbone, and Margaret Bondfield. Sitting here in the 1970s, it's hard to imagine how extraordinarily difficult the position of the first women Members of Parliament must have been. Even many of those men in Parliament who'd been in favour of women's suffrage regarded women right there in the House of Commons as intruders – and they didn't conceal the fact. In later years, Nancy, Lady Astor, the first woman to take her seat, told innumerable stories about the hostility that greeted her.

ASTOR: I'll tell you what I felt when I first started. I didn't

Documentary broadcast on 14 January 1972.

mind the election at all because I liked that, but to walk up the House of Commons between Arthur Balfour and Lloyd George, both of whom had said they believed in women but who would rather have had a rattlesnake in the House than me at the time – they all felt that way – it was very alarming. Do you know sometimes I would sit five hours in that House rather than get out of my seat and walk down?

KING: It wasn't as though Lady Astor was a red or a militant suffragette. Far from it, she was a Conservative and a well-known and highly popular figure in London society. But it made no difference – certainly not to Winston Churchill.

ASTOR: I remember Winston Churchill, you see. He said to me once . . . I've got to say that my best friends couldn't speak to me, they really couldn't, not in the House, and I met him at a dinner about two years afterwards and he said 'It's a very remarkable performance' and I said 'What?' and he said 'Your staying where you are' and I said 'Well Winston, why on earth didn't you speak to me?' He said 'We hoped to freeze you out' and then he added: 'When you entered the House of Commons, I felt like a woman had entered my bathroom and I had nothing to protect myself with except a sponge.'

KING: To this day the Palace of Westminster has the air of a men's club about it, and of course the number of women M.P.s is still very small. But in fact none of the women we talked to admitted to feeling uncomfortable in this masculine atmosphere. Margaret Thatcher puts it this way:

THATCHER: No, I don't find it uncomfortable. I think perhaps we could do with a few more women and then each one of us would be less conspicuous. Sometimes I go into the House, and there are only about twenty-five or twenty-six women Members of Parliament at the moment. We're all very hard workers and often working hard outside the chamber. I go into the House and look round and there are perhaps only three or four, or even fewer women there, then I think: 'Well I simply must stay and sit on the bench a little bit longer, because what will the people in the Gallery think, "Good heavens there are no women in this House" '? So you are conspicuous either by your presence or absence when there are only a few of you.

KING: And Dame Patricia Hornsby-Smith, who's been in Parliament, apart from one break, since 1950, feels much the same way.

HORNSBY-SMITH: There are still Members of the House who will incline to the men's club attitude and, of course, it was a tremendous breakthrough when women first dared to go into the Smoking Room. I can remember asking the late Florence Horsburgh's advice when I first came in, and she said: 'Well, I've made this rule for myself, I have every right to go in, but I know the prejudice and I therefore only go in if I'm escorted,' and after a lively debate one night my minister, who was certainly one of the veteran and most respected Members of the House, the late Lord Crookshank, Harry Crookshank as he then was, said 'You deserve a drink after that,' and swept me into the Smoking Room. There were a few raised eyebrows, but that was it. If Harry Crookshank could take me in, I was accepted.

KING: You might have thought there'd be some temptation for the few women in the House to be self-consciously feminine, to make the point that they *are* women. Lady Astor could certainly remember one such.

ASTOR: She came, she was beautifully dressed, I can't tell you how well she dressed, but dressed for Ascot, not for the House of Commons. And this is the funny thing: I, you know, never changed my garment, I wore a coat and skirt and white shirt, because I said I was going to wear what any woman could wear, and really, as a matter of fact, it looked smarter; but this other lady had a new dress on nearly every day and was flirtatious. You see you can't be flirtatious, men don't like flirting in public. If I'd been a sexy woman, I wouldn't have stayed there a week.

KING: Shirley Williams, an M.P. since 1964 and a junior minister when Labour was in power, is conscious of how much things must have changed since the war.

WILLIAMS: I think that probably was truer in the past: that women had to do one of two things: they either had to be terribly tough – you know, kind of dragons of debate – or else they had to be rather kittenish. I think what's tended to happen since the war has been an acceptance of women just as working colleagues – that's perhaps a bit dull – but it's an easier set-up to work in. What you do find a bit, I think, among some of the older Members is still a slight tone of patronage, and I think among some of the younger Members an obvious wish that there were rather more women in the House and that they were younger.

KING: Far from accepting that women M.P.s go out of their

way to be especially feminine, Margaret Thatcher insists it's really rather the reverse.

THATCHER: When there is criticism of myself, it's not that one is self-consciously feminine, it is that one presents a logical case, fully documented, fully backed up by figures, really tries to bend over backwards in the opposite direction – indeed, I probably present a more reasoned and reasonable case than many of my male colleagues. One of the things being in politics has taught me is that men are not a reasoned or reasonable sex.

KING: Mrs Thatcher generalising about men. But, generalising about women: are there things about female politicians that differentiate them from male politicians – apart from the simple fact of their being women? Barbara Castle is clear that there are.

CASTLE: Yes, I think there are two characteristics you need to succeed – not only in politics but in any kind of major job of responsibility. One is a completely professional attitude to your work. It mustn't be just a stop-gap or a hobby or pin-money work, you must have as passionate an interest in your work as a man does. Now a man can love his family very dearly but still say: 'Sorry darling, the job demands.' My husband as a journalist used to say that many a time; we'd never know whether he would be home Christmas Eve for instance, and he'd have to work nights or stay late at the office, and his family accepted that. Now a woman has got to say the same sort of things to her family. And secondly, you have got to be totally indifferent to jibes or laughter or criticism. It's no good going along and saying: 'Well now, don't be unkind to me, you're hurting my feelings, you be chivalrous.' One of the most flattering things ever said about me by a lobby correspondent writing about the House of Commons was: 'She asks no quarter and she gives none.' Now if you see that quality in a woman politician you will find the House respects them even when it disagrees with them. I think of one outstanding example on the other side of the House, Dame Irene Ward. Now every time she gets up in the House she may get barracking and jeers and the rest of it, she just doesn't give a damn. She just goes ahead if she's got something to say and says it.

KING: Mrs Castle went on to speak of a streak of diffidence in women, and Margaret Thatcher agrees.

THATCHER: I think they're less self-confident than men. That's often struck me. I think a number of women would hold back and say 'I don't know enough about it' when on the same amount of knowledge a man would jump in and make quite an inflamed and passionate speech about it, and he would know no more relevant facts than the woman who refused to make a speech.

KING: There was one point, one that may surprise some listeners, that everybody we talked to was agreed on – emphatically so. Dame Patricia Hornsby-Smith.

HORNSBY-SMITH: I think all the women Members of the House of Commons are amongst the top bracket of hard workers, whether it's dealing with their mail, whether it's going to their constituency, and I think the same applies in business. We know we're going into a world where, if we fail, they will say 'What do you expect with a woman?', and we do tend to flog into it and we do tend to show that we can take the pace and can do the work of Members.

KING: Shirley Williams agrees that this is the most striking difference between women and men politicians, but suspects there are two sides to it.

WILLIAMS: I think that on the whole women are excessively conscientious. I think that they are probably too conscientious and this is why you get letter after letter – and all the other women M.P.s I know do too – which begins by saying 'I am writing to you as a woman M.P.', and the reason is that they suspect they'll get a reply; even if the person writing is not from the woman M.P.'s own constiuency, they are a good deal more likely to get a reply. And the other thing that goes with that, the other side of the medal, is that we tend to be under stress, to show less humour than men do. I think in a way the two things go together and that it's more difficult for a woman than for a man to maintain a balance of, as it were, one's obligations against one's other sorts of enjoyment in life. That ought to change, but it's a feature of the minority and I think it's also true of other minorities, like coloured minorities and so on, in similar situations.

KING: One of the accusations occasionally levelled against women in politics is that, like women drivers, they're indecisive, they dither. Mrs Thatcher was clearly taken aback at the suggestion.

THATCHER: I've never heard that said of women who have got to the top in ministries. I don't think you would ever have said Barbara Castle was indecisive or that she was not a sticker. I don't think you could accuse me of being indecisive. I determined that I was going to keep educational expenditure intact and that if I had to make cuts they would fall on one or two of the welfare things for which I thought people could quite well pay, and indeed which had been cut in the past and, having decided, I haven't retreated either. The retreat from decisions hasn't been from me at all.

KING: When I put it to them that women in politics are apt to be – well – rather bitchy, the M.P.s were more amused than annoyed. 'So', I said to Mrs Williams, 'you would explicitly deny that women politicians are bitchier than men.'

WILLIAMS: Explicitly deny it. That has been the absolute contrary of my own experience.

KING: Pat Hornsby-Smith claims that, if anything, the pull is in the opposite direction.

HORNSBY-SMITH: There's a terrific camaraderie amongst the lady Members, probably cemented by the fact that we know we're in a men's world. I don't think they are bitchy, and certainly as far as jealousy's concerned that's by no means a woman's prerogative.

KING: You mentioned that there is this sense of camaraderie: there is, is there, a sort of informal women's club inside the House of Commons that cuts across party lines?

HORNSBY-SMITH: Well, you see when we had so few women in the House they only gave us one room and we were all slung in together willy-nilly, whereas the men in such accommodation as is available tend to have a Labour group here or a Conservative group there. From the start we've shared rooms across party lines.

KING: Shirley Williams doesn't disagree but stresses how informal it all is.

WILLIAMS: What there is, I think, is a slight sense of solidarity only in this limited way: that we are all anxious that we don't show one another up as foolish. In other words, we are slightly conscious of being a bit of a beleaguered minority and therefore I remember when I made my maiden speech – and I think this is often true of other women M.P.s – a number of other women drifted in from the other party to hear the maiden speech, not because they were interested in me, but because they wanted to make sure that they'd got a woman in the House who wasn't going to be, you know, silly, and I think one is anxious that other women do rather well. In fact, it's very much the opposite of the picture of us all tearing each other's eyes out.

KING: The people who are really conscious of women Members as women, according to Barbara Castle, are their male colleagues. 'Do you feel that when a woman is making a speech from the other side of the House that somehow you think of her as a woman as well as as a Tory?'

CASTLE: No, I don't think one does. I think the men do. I think the men still think of us as women, you know, and you'll hear uncomplimentary remarks under their breath, from both sides of the House, which are made because one is a woman. I think the attitude of the women Members in the House towards each other is a bit divided. On the one hand, there is a kind of solidarity – after all, you have a Lady Members' Retiring Room, you've got to have some place where you can go and kick your shoes off and put your feet up without the chaps around, and change your dresses and so on, and that gives you a kind of solidarity; it's our equivalent, if you like, of the masculine-dominated Smoke Room. But, on the other hand, women bitterly resent it if Mr Speaker tries to match a woman with a woman. I once went to the Speaker – this was when I was a backbencher – and said I wanted urgently to speak in the debate and he said 'Well I've just called a woman from your side' so I said 'What on earth has that got to do with it?' Or he might deliberately, suddenly – I'm not talking about the current Speaker, this is some time ago – but I remember one of them had an infuriating habit, if he called a woman from one side, he would call a woman from the other. I don't want to get up in the House of Commons and answer a woman, I want to get up and answer an argument, possibly an argument that a man's made.

KING: The first woman to take her seat in Parliament was Nancy Astor in 1919. The first woman to be appointed a minister was Margaret Bondfield five years later. Miss Bondfield was also the first woman to enter the Cabinet, in 1929, when she became Minister of Labour. Before going into politics she'd been a trade union official, and in this recording made just before the war she describes how she made the transition.

BONDFIELD: In my trade union and political work I have been

spared the pain of indecision, and have never felt the impulse to turn away from larger responsibilities because the road I travelled just naturally led into wider fields of service. Of course this illustrates my own limitations, of which I'm very conscious – the valuable qualities of curiosity, of criticism and introspection are almost entirely lacking, but I have a natural inclination for teamwork I think, so that, for example, when I am asked if I felt nervous on becoming a Cabinet minister I can truthfully say 'No', because it presented itself as only another and rather wider aspect of work I had been doing for thirty years, and largely with the same team.

KING: All four of the present M.P.s we talked to have also been ministers – two inside the Cabinet, two out. I wondered whether Margaret Thatcher had ever found it awkward dealing with mainly male civil servants, and indeed mainly male Cabinet colleagues.

THATCHER: No, never. I've always found them extremely courteous; but I've been in departments which have been used to dealing with women, though I've dealt with other departments, negotiating with them. I have never found it difficult.

KING: You say they've been extremely courteous, but have they also been prepared to take your decisions as a minister as decisions and that's the end of it?

THATCHER: They've had no option.

KING: I asked Shirley Williams whether she'd ever found it awkward having to order men about.

WILLIAMS: No, I don't think that's awkward. I think it's all a matter of how you do it really; it's perhaps a bit awkward to order them about, but there are ways and ways of making your wishes known. I think the main difficulty frankly was that they just forgot to do things like carrying safety pins if your hem suddenly came down, or remembering that, you know, that you did occasionally have calls of nature, and this is really the only embarrassment about being a woman minister in an almost wholly male ministry: that they just tend to forget that as a woman you do have different needs than a man has, and you have to make these rather clear: you just have to get unembarrassed about it and say: 'Excuse me, are you carrying a safety pin because I have just trod on my hem?'

KING: Barbara Castle described her experiences in government departments, and we then talked about the question of traditional women's subjects in politics.

CASTLE: One undoubtedly felt the first time one walked into the department a stony polite male resistance among one's civil servants. And you know they used to be clearly annoyed about such things as having to have an entirely new lavatory built for the minister because she was a woman and not a man and that kind of thing. The Permanent Secretary in my first department, the Ministry of Overseas Development, told me frankly afterwards that he once said to his wife he'd never work under a woman minister, and yet when I was moved we were the closest of friends and he was heart-broken that I was going.

KING: How had you brought this about? How had you coped with the situation?

CASTLE: Oh by . . . by refusing to let them think of this woman/man relationship – just by behaving like any other minister.

KING: You've had a variety of jobs – Overseas Development, Transport, Labour. None of these have been traditionally thought of as women's subjects. Did you ever feel under any pressure to take up the traditional women's subjects – pensions and education and so on?

CASTLE: Oh no, on the contrary, from the very moment I started in public life, which was on a local authority in London, I said: 'I don't want the traditional women's fields'. Of course they tried to put me on Maternity and Child Welfare and I said: 'I'm not married, and I haven't any children' – that was way back of course – 'and a lot of you chaps are both, so you go on the Maternity and Child Welfare Committee. I want to go on Highways, Sewers and Public Works because I think it's fascinating.'

KING: But Mrs Castle is something of an exception. The record shows that, since the time of Margaret Bondfield, women have held altogether forty-nine posts involving the running of government departments, and no less than thirty-three of these forty-nine have been in a limited range of social service fields – nine in education, nine in pensions, and so on. No woman has ever been at the Ministry of Defence, only one each at the Board of Trade and the Foreign Office, and only one, Mrs Castle herself, at Transport. Margaret Thatcher is the third woman to hold office as Minister of Education. Has she felt in her political career that there was some pressure on her to specialise in the so-called women's subjects?

THATCHER: It isn't so much pressure on you. You could deal with pressure. I think it's even more deep-rooted than that. It is expected of you that you will go to the subjects which are expected to be of most interest to women, that is, things which concern the family and children. And I started my career in the Ministry of National Insurance as Parliamentary Secretary to the Minister of Pensions, and I followed another woman – Dame Patricia Hornsby-Smith – and she'd followed one, I think – Dame Edith Pitt – so you see that that was expected to be a woman's job. And it took quite some time to break out of that, although it's interesting to think that in the early days, you know, women didn't go to those departments. The first woman Cabinet minister was Minister of Labour.

KING: Have you ever felt yourself tempted not to live up to other people's expectations of you as a woman, and perhaps to specialise in foreign affairs or trade and industry? You have, in fact, been a spokesman on these subjects.

THATCHER: I have been a spokesman on the Treasury, I've been a spokesman on Transport, I've been a spokesman on Fuel and Power, because I happen also to have a technical degree and also have been a lawyer, so I don't reckon that my interests are confined to subjects which are expected to be of interest to women.

KING: Pat Hornsby-Smith reckons that the position in this connection has changed quite dramatically over the last twenty years or so.

HORNSBY-SMITH: When I went in in 1950 women were only expected to speak on social welfare, education, housing, insurance, health, and you were looked at askance if you tried to speak in a foreign affairs debate, or any of the industrial debates. But that has very very substantially changed, and it's much easier now to specialise and attend and participate in the various party and other committees on subjects which are not specifically social welfare.

KING: Shirley Williams also thinks that women have broken out of this particular mould. She gives a good deal of the credit to her former chief Harold Wilson.

WILLIAMS: It's always been the case that women have tended to be put into the social services or education. The statutory woman always ends up in those fields, and I think historically almost everyone has, except for Margaret Bondfield briefly in Labour, all the others have been in those fields. And really I think it would have gone on like that had Wilson not taken the fairly bold step of putting Mrs Castle in at Overseas Aid, and then subsequently Transport, which most people would think of as a man's job. And now I think the only one that would be thought to be a bit way-out would be Defence.

KING: Harold Wilson as Prime Minister undoubtedly made a big difference. One has only to look at the reference books. He appointed far more women ministers than any other Prime Minister has ever done, and appointed them to a far wider range of offices. Barbara Castle feels rather strongly on this point, and I asked her whether she felt as a woman that her promotion prospects, before she entered government in 1964, were better or worse than those of a man of equal standing and ability.

CASTLE: Worse, undoubtedly. All my political life I have felt that, other things being equal, a woman has a worse chance of promotion, because there's got to be a positive mental effort by a man to accept that the woman is good, whereas it's taken for granted among his male colleagues – 'Bright chap, of course he should be promoted.' And the person who really did make a dramatic breakthrough was Harold Wilson. I think this is one of the things he'll go down in history for, because you see at that time when we were in power there were some eighteen women – Labour women Members, I think I'm right in saying, in the House. Now, Harold made eight of them ministers of different ranks – not all in the Cabinet, of course, some were only junior ministers. But that's a very high proportion. And he did it, not to get the woman's vote – because you could do that with your statutory woman, you know – he did it because he doesn't feel the need to make that extra positive effort of appreciating women. He has very great respect for women. It delights him giving them opportunities, and he is even more delighted when they justify his choice.

KING: Did Margaret Thatcher ever feel, before she entered the Cabinet, that her prospects for promotion were less good because she was a woman?

THATCHER: Yes, I think to some extent one did. To some extent one does feel that life at the top is very much a man's club, and it was therefore quite a step to go into the Cabinet. And also I've always felt – and I'm sure you'd probably agree – that there are some jobs in politics which women will never hold; some of us would never wish to hold them. For example, you'll never have a woman Minister of Defence.

KING: Won't you ever have a woman Prime Minister?

THATCHER: Well, it's possible, but I don't think it will come for many many years. I don't think it'll come in my lifetime.

KING: All of the women we've been talking to actually made it. They got selected as candidates and they became M.P.s. But, as Margaret Thatcher said earlier on, there are still only twenty-six women Members of the House. Part of the explanation is that not many women even try to get into national politics. Why not? Shirley Williams.

WILLIAMS: Well, I suppose partly because it's seen to be, or believed to be, a very tough profession. Of course an awful lot of women do try local government as distinct from national politics. I think secondly because the timetable is extremely difficult, involving as it does a lot of evening work. And I think thirdly because there isn't any very clear career structure. A lot of people go into the House who've been lawyers or journalists. They move in from other professions, and these are also professions in which women tend not to be in very large numbers.

KING: Mrs Thatcher added two more reasons.

THATCHER: The majority of women get married and have a family. While the children are young they obviously would wish to be at home with them, and also they find it difficult to get someone reliable to be with the children even if they themselves want to be away from home. So that's one very obvious reason, and after that, of course, they'd have a gap between their ambitions and perhaps being able to fulfil them. And the second reason is related to it; it really is geography. Not many women looking after a family can, say, come up from Leeds, or Exeter, or down from Glasgow to be in London for the greater part of the week. Now this restricts the number of starters, and really restricts it to those whose family either are almost grown up, or who live near London, or who perhaps have an aunt or grandma who can take care of the children while they're away from home themselves.

KING: But it's not just that relatively few women try to get into the House: most of those who do try fail. This is also true of men, of course, but is there a specific prejudice against women amongst the local party activists who select candidates? Pat Hornsby-Smith complained that it's terribly difficult to get the local associations to accept a woman. 'Do you think there's simple prejudice on the part of selectors?'

HORNSBY-SMITH: Oh yes. They go through the motions now – there was a time when they said no women will be considered. But now, if they get two or three hundred names, they seem to manage to eliminate them before they get to the short-list, so that a woman is neither seen nor heard even if her qualifications on paper are acknowledgedly better than some of the men's.

KING: Why do you think this is? Is it that the people making the selection think that the voters themselves will not vote for a woman candidate?

HORNSBY-SMITH: To an extent yes, but it's not only on the men's side. There are a lot of women who feel that they'd rather be represented by a man. And, of course, when they get a man, particularly if he's married, they think they're getting two for the price of one, and whereas the political wife is a golden asset to the M.P. husband and gets credit for him when she goes to the coffee mornings and the fêtes, if you're a spinster like myself you've got to be there personally or else. Alternatively, the married woman M.P. can hardly send her husband hacking round for her.

KING: Barbara Castle was equally clear that there was prejudice amongst the selectors, but she had a rather different idea about where it was to be found:

CASTLE: Among the men on the selection committees. I stress the word 'men' because I know there is a current myth – I met it when I was trying to get into Parliament way back in '44 – I met it myself. I used to be told by all the men in the party: 'Now look here Barbara, well I think you ought to be in the House, but women won't vote for women.' You know, that hoary old one you always get. And my experience is the exact opposite, and I'm only in Parliament because the women in my local constituency party insisted on having a woman shortlisted. I was lucky, because at that time Blackburn was a two-Member constituency – double-barrelled as we used to call them – and so they selected two. They satisfied their male prejudice by selecting a man, and then having a second vote they said: 'Oh we like that girl, we'll have her.'

KING: Shirley Williams is the only one who can't really recall encountering hostility at selection conferences.

WILLIAMS: No, I don't think there's a lot of prejudice at a selection conference – not at a Labour one. In fact, it can work slightly the other way in the sense that people feel there ought to be a woman on the list. I believe, though others may disagree with this, that there is some prejudice at a Conservative selection conference against women. I don't think that's true of a Labour selection conference, no. The difficulty is much more often that very few women appear.

KING: Margaret Thatcher is clear that voters aren't hostile to women candidates.

THATCHER: I think when it comes to a general election the vote goes very much more on party lines, but once you're known and your work is known they look at you really as a person, or as a personality, and not according to your sex, or your family commitments.

KING: This is one topic on which we thought we should get the views of an outside expert, because the women, after all, have an interest in holding the views they do. I asked David Butler of Nuffield College, Oxford, whether there's any hard evidence of anti-women feeling amongst the people who select candidates.

BUTLER: I think there is some evidence of this. I've certainly met plenty of people who say: 'Look, I'm not prejudiced against women.' And equally they say: 'I'm not prejudiced against Jews, against Catholics, or other kinds of people who might cause prejudice in others. But we've got to be careful. This is a marginal seat and we want to get as big a vote as we can. And if you have a woman it might cause prejudice. Women don't like women,' they say, 'and therefore it's better not to take a chance, let's play safe.'

KING: David Butler then made a much more arresting point: that the quality of the women trying to break into politics isn't all that high.

BUTLER: I mean, I have known of people who've been very

much actively interested in getting more women candidates and saying: 'The difficulty is they aren't very good.' If you are actually going to choose on merit, not in relation to sex at all, but just on merit, how many really good women candidates are there? Actually the number of qualified women is small. I mean, the number of women who are graduates – higher education is a qualification – and the number of women with business experience is much smaller than the number of men. And that's why they have less of a chance.

KING: Apart from the business of candidate selection, what about the voters? Does David Butler think they're prejudiced against women?

BUTLER: I don't think there is any solid evidence to that effect at all. There is no reason to suppose the swing has been greater against women when a woman has replaced a man. There is really nothing that I have seen – and I must say it's not been a matter that's been studied in any particular detail and it's not one that's very easy to study – but such evidence as there is is wholly negative. They're not influenced by candidates at all, I mean tall, short, dark, handsome, clever, stupid, male, female.

KING: So far we've skirted round one of the main things most people think about when they consider women in politics. How does a woman M.P. reconcile her commitment to her husband and children with her commitment to politics? Lady Astor was lucky: she was enormously rich and could afford to have her six children tutored privately or sent to the best boarding-schools. At any rate the children don't seem to have minded too much.

ASTOR: One of my children said when he was at Eton – that was at a time when I was conspicuous: 'Lady Astor does this and that' – and this other boy said to my son: 'It must be terrible having your mother in the House of Commons.' And he said: 'Yes, it's bad but if she wasn't there she'd probably be in the Salvation Army and that would be worse.'

KING: Of course not all women M.P.s have family commitments. Does Dame Patricia Hornsby-Smith think that being single has helped or hindered her in politics?

HORNSBY-SMITH: Well, it's enabled me to give much more time to the job because I've no one to nag me and say 'You haven't been home for a meal for three weeks and this is the fifth consecutive weekend you've been away', so to that extent it is an advantage. To the extent that I've still got all my chores and my flat to run and all my own fetching and chasing to do, it's a liability not to have someone to aid one.

KING: Barbara Castle, who's been married since those days on the local council in London, thinks it's marvellous that people are marrying younger.

CASTLE: There is a tremendous interest in family life. I've a very great interest in family life myself and I don't think you have to sacrifice family life to get the zest for politics. But it does mean there are very great physical difficulties for women; you see, when you are in the House of Commons it can make terrific demands on your time and on your priorities. As you know, my husband has been very ill and it's been an extremely difficult period fulfilling my duties in the House, which I have done, and at the same time not neglecting him; but these are additional barriers a woman has.

KING: Mrs Thatcher has a husband and two children; how does she overcome these barriers? She has said in public that, in fact, she'd find it difficult to carry on in politics without a family behind her.

THATCHER: I think it's always important that you should have a refuge to which you can go; somewhere where you can go and be absolutely certain of unconditional affection and unconditional loyalty. And, you know, you do have to take quite a lot of knocks, but when you can get home and you have both those things then you realise perhaps what's important in life.

KING: How do you cope with what one might call the managerial problems of running both a department and a home at the same time?

THATCHER: You just have to be extremely active, extremely fit, and a reasonably good organiser. And you must recognise that you live at about twice the pace of anyone else.

KING: Mrs Thatcher said when we were chatting afterwards that it's mainly a matter of organisation. If it's something you know about in advance, like a child's birthday or a school speech day, then you make sure you're free that day. If it's something like an unexpected illness, then you just have to drop everything and be at home. But then – as she pointed out – family crises are also a part of men's lives. President Kennedy, for instance, once had to cancel a meeting with the British Prime Minister because his father was ill. Of course, it does help to have a constituency not too far from the House of Commons.

THATCHER: I could always dash quickly from Westminster – I have a constituency near London – from Westminster to the constituency and then home. I've lived life on a very, very small triangle; otherwise I just couldn't have coped.

KING: Towards the beginning of the programme, some complimentary remarks were made about Dame Irene Ward, the longest-serving woman M.P. – the Mother of the House as you might say. Who are the women members who've been most admired by their female colleagues? Shirley Williams.

WILLIAMS: Before I got in the House of Commons, one of the people I most admired was Eleanor Rathbone, who brought in family allowances, a marvellous woman, a sort of pure flame. Since I've been in the House: Barbara Castle who I admire immensely for her courage – she's one of the bravest people I've ever met, I think – and her kind of derring-do, if I can put it like that, and the sort of sheer flair that she brings to things.

KING: Characteristics that are often attributed to men, in fact.

WILLIAMS: Characteristics often attributed to men.

KING: Eleanor Rathbone, the first person mentioned by Mrs Williams, probably rings only a very faint bell, if any, in the minds of most people. She was an Independent Member during the 1930s and a formidable campaigner against Chamberlain's appeasement policy; in favour of the enfranchisement of women in India; for Zionism; for the better treatment of refugees and aliens. As Shirley Williams says, she was a sort of pure flame. The luminous quality of that flame can still be heard in this recording of one of her speeches:

RATHBONE: These feminist reforms are not, I think, what we enfranchised women prize most highly: we care even more for the opportunities our citizenship gives us of taking a full part in the life of our nation. But in doing our feminist work we acquired an expertise which many of us have applied successfully in other walks of life. Reasonable argument there must always be, but there must also be the passion of conviction and the fire of enthusiasm. It's been the good fortune of the women's movement to have had among its leaders and its rank and file many women who combine these attributes of reason and of passion.

KING: Margaret Thatcher picked out two women she particularly admires, one from each side of the House. The Conservative again, Dame Irene Ward.

THATCHER: She is a doughty fighter without being a bluestocking. She's a tremendously sturdy personality; she never misses a chance; she's known and respected wherever she goes in the world and she's quite unique. And she also – it's interesting to watch her – she also knows every nuance of procedure in the House of Commons, she can use every situation to advantage instantly; and I must confess, you know, Irene does sometimes get away with things that no one else could because we all say 'Oh well, it's Irene'. But the women say it just as much as the men.

KING: Mrs Thatcher's choice on the Labour side: another doughty fighter, Barbara Castle.

THATCHER: I do admire her, she's very tenacious, she's extremely hard-working and I think she was very, very unfairly treated by her own party when she didn't get the vote to go into the Shadow Cabinet although I'm very pleased she's been put in. But again, you see, and it's just an example of what I was saying earlier, she was decisive, she was a sticker and because she was both of those things she lost out.

KING: But, all that having been said, perhaps the central question about women in politics is this: do women in politics really make a difference? Do they contribute to political life in any way that's uniquely their own? After all, one can imagine a Parliament with only men; women weren't permitted to sit in Parliament in Switzerland until last year. Shirley Williams.

WILLIAMS: I think probably it isn't so much the case that women politicians as such contribute something special. I think what's more true is that the whole of the women's vote and the representation of women by women has essentially moved the whole field of what you might call family problems, welfare problems, and so on, to the centre of politics, and I very much doubt if that would have happened without this massive move of women into politics as voters as much as Members of Parliament.

KING: Barbara Castle sees it as that, but also as something wider. How would government have been different without women?

CASTLE: I think our social life in this country would have been different. You see, women have to some extent specialised on women's questions, but their biggest contribution to the rights of women really does exist in being there and obviously having a right on merit to be there. That alters male attitudes; it alters attitudes in government. That, accompanied by the fact we've all of us had a bash at some little injustice against women, whether it's as small as my turnstile campaign or as great as some maternity and child welfare issues.

KING: Or as equal pay.

CASTLE: Or as equal pay indeed. And that is going to be followed by Willie Hamilton's Bill to outlaw discrimination against women in employment.

KING: Now what about equal pay. Do you think that a man in your job when you were at the Department of Employment and Productivity would have been inclined to press as hard on that particular issue?

CASTLE: No, I don't. I think there is no doubt that we wouldn't have got – I wouldn't have got – the policy through Cabinet at a time of great economic difficulty if I hadn't been a woman and therefore cared passionately about it.

KING: I said right at the beginning that this programme wasn't going to be concerned with defending women's role in politics. Even so, if anybody at the beginning still had any doubts on the matter, I hope they've been laid to rest. Not just by the record of the things women have accomplished in politics, but by the undoubted calibre of the women who've contributed to the programme.

6 The Westminster Lobby Correspondents

This programme, for a change, is not about politicians, but about the people who write about politics: the hundred or so journalists who cover Westminster and Downing Street, the lobby correspondents. The Lobby produces practically all the political news we all consume, yet almost nothing is known by the general public about how it actually works. And even among journalists there are profoundly divergent views about whether the Lobby in its present form is a good thing or not. Anthony Howard, the Editor of the *New Statesman*, who for years has been the scourge of the Lobby:

HOWARD: It's far too cosy. Politicians and journalists live in each other's pockets under the system, and I often think probably they're only talking to each other as well. No other country, I think, has quite the same incestuous relationship as we have between parliamentarians and correspondents at Westminster. I've always said, you know, that it's almost like Piccadilly before the Wolfenden Report: there stand the lobby correspondents waiting, soliciting, for the politician to come out; they treat them as if they were their clients and, you know, in some ways I think the fact has to be faced that lobby correspondents do become instruments for a politician's gratification.

KING: Against this David Wood, the lobby correspondent of *The Times*:

WOOD: Generally speaking, I do not know of any group of journalists who, on the whole – and I'm not saying we're never without sinners by any means, any more than any other branch of the trade is – I don't know of any branch of the trade where, at any rate, they aim more consistently at a high standard than in the Westminster Lobby.

Documentary broadcast on 3 June 1972.

KING: We'll return to these different assessments of the Lobby later on, but before we do, the facts: what is the Lobby? How does it work? The name is easy to explain. Members of the Lobby, unlike ordinary members of the general public, can circulate freely in most parts of the Palace of Westminster – most notably in the Members' Lobby itself.

Much of the work of lobby correspondents is like the work of other journalists; but there are two special features of Lobby journalism that the newspaper reader ought to be aware of. The first is that Lobby journalists are under a strict obligation not to reveal the sources of their stories. There's a formal set of Lobby Rules which says that it's the lobby correspondent's 'primary duty to protect his informants, and care must be taken not to reveal anything that could lead to their identification'. In other words if, say, a Tory M.P. tells a reporter that he and some friends of his are about to vote against the Government, the reporter can publish the fact that a revolt is about to take place, but he mustn't identify the M.P. who told him.

The second thing about Lobby journalism is that members of the Lobby attend frequent briefings, given by ministers and other Government and Opposition spokesmen. These are not press conferences in the ordinary sense. Not only are the reporters present not supposed, in the usual way, to reveal their sources, but the fact that such briefings take place at all is supposed to be kept a secret. Indeed, a great deal of the Lobby's work used to be shrouded in an atmosphere of semi-secrecy, rather like the rites of a Masonic Lodge. One or two Lobby men weren't very happy when they discovered we were going to do this programme.

One set of regular Lobby briefings is given by the Prime Minister's press spokesman. Sir Harold Evans, who served at No. 10 for seven years under Harold Macmillan, describes what takes place.

EVANS: It happened customarily twice a day. There was a morning meeting, which was usually quite thinly attended because it was the evening papers and the agencies only. The spokesman always took those meetings. In the afternoon, one met at the House and that was a fuller meeting usually because the full Lobby would turn up for that. After one had talked to the Lobby at their two meetings during the day, one naturally expected to have follow-up questions from individuals, and one had to be available right through the evening and indeed often into the small hours if anything important was moving. At the weekends one also had to be ready to deal with individual inquiries. This was roughly the pattern of it.

KING: Was the attendance at the actual briefings fairly constant, or did you get more people when there was some really hot news around?

EVANS: Oh, there were always more people when there was really hot news. Of course the Lobby, being in daily contact and having the sense of the way things were moving, always knew when there was anything of significance and the attendance would go up and down quite a bit.

KING: How long did the Downing Street meeting last?

EVANS: Again, it would depend on what was happening. If one had a lot to say, well obviously, that would breed a lot of questions and it would go on for perhaps three-quarters of an hour or even an hour. On the other hand, if it was absolutely straightforward and routine, it might last, in a desultory kind of way, perhaps twenty minutes.

KING: What sort of information was given out at the briefings? What sorts of things were you trying to put across?

EVANS: Well, there was always, to begin with, a great interest obviously in what the Prime Minister was doing: his actual activities and his rota of meetings, and one would therefore probably start with that kind of information which would lead to questioning about particular engagements and events. Sometimes, of course, one would have a particular piece of information about a development in policy or something of that kind and then you'd tell the Lobby this and they would question you about it.

KING: The other main briefings are given on Thursday afternoons by the Leader of the House and, separately, by the Leader of the Opposition. John Whale of the *Sunday Times* describes the little turret room at Westminster where they take place.

WHALE: It's a dingy chamber about twenty feet square, overlooking on one side the Thames, from a considerable height, and on another side the leads of the roof of the Palace of Westminster. It has, on the walls, boards rather of the kind that you see in the gymnasia of boarding-schools recording past office-bearers of the Lobby, and it has enough chairs to seat pretty well the whole of the Lobby which now must number up to a hundred people.

KING: I asked Sir Harold Evans how these Thursday briefings differed from the ones Downing Street was responsible for.

EVANS: This was really a ministers' Lobby meeting and the Leader of the House, having gone through the business of the week, had an awful lot to talk about, usually, and on matters of depth and substance. And, since the Leader of the House is usually a top figure in Government, obviously the Lobby were very keen to probe him.

KING: And similarly on the Opposition side. Such briefings are important and they're worth describing because most people aren't aware they take place at all. But, still, they cannot take up much of the time even of a Lobby man who attends them regularly. David Wood has been in the Lobby for *The Times* for over fifteen years. He discussed with me how he spends an ordinary working day.

WOOD: I start my day by most people's standards rather late – that's to say, I'm not really conscious until about nine o'clock because I've worked late the night before as a rule. I then read the . . . no, that's not quite true. I was going to say I read the papers. In fact I skim the papers and read the leading articles. I then usually turn to some White Paper, Blue Book or a copy of *Hansard*, when I want to catch up on something I've missed.

KING: Do you do this at home or in the office?

WOOD: I do this at home, in trains, and wherever I find myself.

KING: Does reading the morning papers and other documents take up most of the morning?

WOOD: Oh, by no means – no. You get telephone calls – some from your office, some from your friends, some from those who were your friends yesterday but are not after breakfast-time this morning. And the mornings really are quite active until you move off, about eleven o'clock, and then the day begins. Meeting people, talking, being talked at.

KING: These friends and former friends, are they mainly politicians?

WOOD: Yes. In this trade you make friends over the years and, of course, you have to write things, or your paper chooses to publish things not written by you, which rub the bloom off the peach for a few days or a week possibly. They don't want to be so friendly with you as they were before; but of course eventually they find that you or your paper has published something with which they passionately agree and they are then once again your warm friends. Political friendships, in this curious love/hate relationship between the Lobby and politicians, are very durable. It's astonishing how much stick we can take from politicians and how much they are prepared to take from us.

KING: That latter part of the morning, do you spend it in your office at *The Times* or at the Palace of Westminster or where?

WOOD: I go to *The Times* building only for conferences and lunches and for special occasions, festivities, gala days and the delivery of copy. Apart from that I prefer to work in a teashop. I say teashop. It's sometimes rather more luxurious than that, but what I mean is I am not accustomed to working in an office in that sense.

KING: Do you reckon normally to have a working lunch? That's to say a lunch with a fellow member of the Lobby or, presumably more commonly, a politician or civil servant?

WOOD: I'd never dream of having lunch with a fellow member of the Lobby. I can think of nothing more depressing. I have lunches, even in the slackest times, at least four days a week and usually five days a week with politicians, ministers usually, sometimes civil servants, sometimes backbenchers who happen at that point of time to be important, or sometimes of course diplomats from abroad or politicians from abroad.

KING: Do you spend much of the day actually in the chamber listening to the debates in the House?

WOOD: This varies enormously. If a Bill is in committee one looks in occasionally to check on the things that you think might be of interest, but generally speaking you'd never dream of spending a great deal of time there. You are keeping check on it elsewhere in the Palace of Westminster.

KING: You do spend additional time in the Palace outside the chamber. Where normally? Roving about or in one particular place?

WOOD: Generally speaking one doesn't – I don't, let me not generalise – I don't spend an awful lot of time in the Members' Lobby itself. I think it's an unfruitful place to be. I think everybody who operates within the Lobby, as I do, keeps a strict limit on the amount of time he spends there. Occasionally you go down there and make appointments with people to meet them elsewhere, where you are not in eyeshot and earshot of other people.

KING: I was going to ask you about that. Generally speaking you do see people by appointment, you don't gather much news just by chance encounters in the corridors?

WOOD: I don't, no. You make arrangements to see them, or for them to telephone you, or you to telephone them.

KING: And you begin to file your copy at about what time of day for the paper?

WOOD: Varies enormously. The office would complain that I begin filing very late. Generally speaking I have not very much to write before six o'clock, and this could go on – it varies with the day – it could go on until eleven, twelve, one, sometimes two.

KING: And you spend your evenings, do you, in much the same way as you do your afternoons? The afternoon and the evening are part of one continuous sequence in your life?

WOOD: I think that would be a mistake. It would suggest that the whole thing is routine. The whole point about the job – and this is the fascination of the job, and it is why you tend to get people serving for many years in it – is that one day is scarcely ever like another, and your time is unpredictable. Sudden squalls blow up and you have to deal with them, or you get a sudden telephone call and, instead of being at the Palace of Westminster, it's obviously more appropriate to be in some restaurant or hotel at a little distance from Westminster where you won't be observed, and so on. The whole thing is unpredictable and non-routine.

KING: You mentioned not being observed. How far do you think it's important to work by yourself and not either with other colleagues on *The Times* or with other members of the Lobby?

WOOD: I'd never dream of working with members of other papers, never have done and never shall. And let's face it, if my friends, my good friends, Walter Terry of the *Daily Mail* and Wilfred Sendall of the *Daily Express*, saw my head coming up for the third time, they'd push it under, and I'd do the same for them. I notice John Whale's book *Journalism and Government* talks about a cartel system whereby the switching of stories between lobby correspondents who are supposed to be rivals takes place. I think this possibly happens where a provincial paper in the North of England has one man and a provincial paper in the South of England has one man. Quite clearly, to compete with the Fleet Street papers who have more than one man, they have to carve up the work, and this is understandable. In this way their papers get a better cover. But I don't know of any Fleet Street man who would dream of giving me a story, nor one who would dream of my giving him one.

KING: As you've probably already guessed David Wood doesn't take the formal Lobby briefings over-seriously. I asked him whether he ever attends the morning briefings at Downing Street.

WOOD: Never, except occasionally during recesses when I can't think of any other way to spend the morning.

KING: Why not?

WOOD: I see no point for me in the morning briefings. As a matter of fact, I am not a very conscientious attender of mass briefings anyway.

KING: But he does find the regular Thursday meetings more useful . . .

WOOD: . . . because they point the way ahead and you can start from that point. You know the dates, you know the names of the people involved, you know the plan for the week ahead, and this is very useful and important information.

KING: The trouble with most briefings, as David Wood says, is that, with so many people involved, they are almost mass meetings. He doesn't rely on them – at least not without further investigation – for information on what the Government is doing. I asked him about what his main sources of information were. His answers were brief, but told one what one wanted to know. 'Do you have much private contact with ministers? Do you see individual Cabinet ministers alone, fairly often?'

WOOD: Yes.

KING: To talk to them about the work of their departments, the general political situation, and so on?

WOOD: Yes. I'm being cryptic . . .

KING: That's the way it looks from the journalist's side of the fence. How does it look from the politician's? I raised with William Deedes, the Conservative Member for Ashford and a former Minister in Charge of Government Information, the same point I raised with David Wood. How much contact is there in the normal way between Cabinet ministers and either the Lobby as a whole or individual members of the Lobby? William Deedes was less cryptic.

DEEDES: That depends a lot on the Cabinet minister. He can always invite, or ask himself to be invited – I think that's the way it has to go – by the Lobby, in order to given them information which he thinks is important to them. Apart from those formal, if private, occasions, how much he encounters individual members of the Lobby around the corridors and in the Lobby is very much up to him. He would probably know at least half of them, and they would take an interest in him. And it really depends on how forthcoming he is disposed to be towards them.

KING: And how often would a minister, say, have lunch or dinner with somebody in the Lobby, or several of them?

DEEDES: Open to any lobby correspondent to invite any minister, any Member of Parliament, to lunch with him. And I think a good deal of very pleasant exchange goes on in this way. It is a very civilised way in which to discuss the work of a department and what ministers may be doing, thinking, contemplating. I think this is a very legitimate activity.

KING: Gerald Kaufman worked for Harold Wilson as the Labour Party's Parliamentary Press Liaison Officer before becoming Labour M.P. for Ardwick. He isn't terribly impressed by the efforts of ministers to use the press. I asked him how far ministers, whether at press conferences or briefings, deliberately tried to create an effect in the next morning's papers.

KAUFMAN: The ministers who are brightest try very hard indeed. I'm afraid, though, that in both the Labour and Conservative Parties there aren't all that many ministers who know how to go about it.

KING: Gerald Kaufman and William Deedes painted similar pictures of the backbencher's relationship with the Lobby. I asked William Deedes: 'How much attention does the Lobby pay to you? Do you find people quite frequently coming up and asking questions or ringing you at home or whatever?'

DEEDES: No, they don't pester people in that way. Generally speaking, they minimise very skilfully the trouble they put Members to. They have to check a certain amount of information and of course they very often like to know what goes on at backbench committee meetings upstairs, which they have every right to try to discover, which Members are encouraged to be discreet about. But that is really part of the give and take of the place. Sometimes they get what they want, sometimes Members are discreet and they don't. But I don't think that's changed much over the years.

KING: From the point of view of the journalist, presumably one of the disadvantages of collecting news around the Palace of Westminster is that it is not a very private place. And that if an M.P. is seen talking to a journalist then the whole world knows about it?

DEEDES: Everything you do in that sense is very public. Everybody can see whom you are talking to. You can, of course, ask people to ring you up. My impression is the Lobby has thinned out a bit. But one imagines that perhaps rather more goes on on the telephone now – and that would not be visible in the way you describe – than actually in interchange between chaps on the floor on the premises.

KING: On the other hand, there is an aspect of the way the Lobby works that can lead to ill-feeling with backbenchers, as Gerald Kaufman explains:

KAUFMAN: What backbenchers do resent, and it's a resentment I share, is that journalists should receive advance copies of parliamentary documents before they do, and should receive advance copies of parliamentary statements before they do. A backbencher finds it awfully difficult to put sensible and probing questions, say, to Sir Alec Douglas-Home when he's made his statement about the Pearce Report if he's neither seen a copy of the Pearce Report nor even seen a copy of Sir Alec's statement, whereas the journalists have both of these in advance and, therefore, when they meet ministers privately – as it's pretty certain they did with Sir Alec – they are able to ask much more probing questions.

KING: So much for what the Lobby is and how it works. We could go into more detail, but the outlines of the system are clear enough. The question is: is it a good system? Does it provide us, the readers of newspapers, with a full, accurate picture of day-to-day political life? Some critics of the Lobby make much of the formal set of Lobby Rules I referred to earlier on. And it must be said that some of the rules do sound pretty peculiar – or at least more suited to a boys' boarding-school than to top-level journalism. 'Don't run,' one of them says, 'after a Minister or Private Member. It's nearly always possible to place oneself in a position to avoid this.' Another reads: 'Don't crowd together in the Lobby so as to be conspicuous. In general, always act with the recollection that you are a guest of Parliament.' This business of being a guest of Parliament is something Anthony Howard particularly objects to.

HOWARD: There is something, it seems to me, inappropriate in journalists accepting a grace and favour position. And what the Lobby really comes down to – and this you are constantly reminded when you work there – is that you are, as it were, a guest of the Speaker in the Palace of Westminster, and you have no rights there. You can't even sit down. When I was first a lobby correspondent – I've never been a full member of the Lobby – and I was a young man of twenty-five or something, I stood in the Lobby and I got rather tired of standing, and I suddenly saw that there was a nice bench, and so I thought: 'Well, I'll go and sit down.' All sort of hell was let loose. Policemen rushed forward and said, 'You can't sit there, you can't sit there, get up.' And, I mean, it . . . it's . . . to talk about, you know, public school atmosphere, it's absolutely absurd.

KING: But one can probably make too much of the formal rules as such. In the course of our investigations we discovered that some lobby correspondents had never even read them. John Whale.

WHALE: Nobody ever showed me the Lobby Rules. Indeed, I didn't know they existed until an academic published them not long ago. I simply turned up and shambled in.

KING: And, when I asked David Wood of *The Times* how much attention he paid to the Lobby Rules, to my considerable astonishment I got the same answer.

WOOD: None at all, because the Lobby Rules, which I read the other day for the first time, on the instructions of a colleague of mine on *The Times* who happens at the moment to be secretary of the Lobby, insisted it was about time after twenty-two years in and out of the Palace of Westminster that I read the rules. I read them and, as I expected, they are, of course, a rather pompous formulation of the normal way in which every newspaper man, every radio and television man, ever operates.

KING: Nevertheless, a number of specific criticisms are made of the way the Lobby operates at the moment, some of them arising directly out of the rules, some of them not. One of the main causes of complaint has to do with the understanding that journalists will not identify the sources of their stories. They say things like 'sources close to the Prime Minister are claiming . . .' when what they mean is 'the Prime Minister's press man told us at the lobby briefing yesterday afternoon'. Anthony Howard is particularly scathing on this point.

HOWARD: What you have now is a system of private signals between the journalist and those of his readers who are in the sort of knowing in-group. They can tell that when he writes 'it was a view in Government circles last night . . .' he's been to see . . . perhaps even know he's been to see the Prime Minister, or he's been to see, let's say, the . . . at least the Chief Whip or something. But the reader has no possible way of knowing this, and so it is a fraud on the public, it is a deception of the newspaper reader. And as the newspaper reader is the person who keeps the paper in business, I think he's entitled to a cleaner and fairer deal.

KING: According to John Whale, whose new book *Journalism and Government* has just been published, the practice of not quoting sources by name leads to more than just the use of an in-group code.

WHALE: The trouble with anonymity is that it can be the mother of invention, or at any rate the mother of exaggeration. One can talk to the departmental press officer and then leave one's readers with the impression, without actually saying so, that one has been talking to a minister. Again and again one can talk, or listen, to the Downing Street press secretary and refer grandly to 'ministers' or 'the quarters that matter', or 'sources in the know', or phrases of this kind, which dignify one's source, give one's readers the impression that they are getting it from a well much higher up the the stream than they are in fact.

KING: I put these points to David Wood. Does he think there's anything to be said for the view that non-attributable interviews, interviews on Lobby terms shouldn't really take place, or at least that their results shouldn't be published? Should you put things in the paper only if you can put a name to them?

WOOD: I should think this is absolutely preposterous. I can't think the people who make this point have any understanding of the way newspapers have their reporting done at all. It applies to every form of journalistic specialism. It applies to defence, to diplomacy, to the labour correspondents, even to the agricultural correspondents. And on occasion I think I've been present at the meetings of nearly all these groups during the last, oh, very nearly thirty years. And they all have to be conducted on the same principle as any reporter anywhere at all works, which is that if you can get more information by not naming names then you get your information that way.

KING: Isn't there a danger, though, that some lobby correspondents at any rate will be tempted to invent a little bit, embroider a little bit, knowing that if there isn't a name attached to the story then nobody can be any the wiser?

WOOD: I think there is a danger here, and it's a danger that runs throughout journalism. I've no doubt that there are occasions now and again in the Westminster Lobby when this does happen. If you are limited for time, if there are only a certain number of informants you can hope to get hold of in a given amount of time – and no newspaper editor is prepared to wait until next week before you write it – and so in this way, of course, error must creep in.

KING: And even John Whale, although unhappy about some of the results of the present system, doesn't see how in this respect it can be changed.

WHALE: Anonymity is sure to persist; even in Washington, notionally the home of open government and an open press, there is a great deal of non-attributable briefing. Indeed, Washington journalists are even freer with cryptic phrases about 'sources in the know' than London journalists are. I think the system is to some extent in the nature of things.

KING: But does the Lobby system as such, with its briefings which most members of the Lobby attend, encourage all of the lobby correspondents to see leading politicians, as it were, through the same eyes? Does it encourage a sort of collective view of politicians? One's told, for example, that Rab Butler in the early fifties came to be a favourite with all of the lobby correpondents because he told such good stories and was so indiscreet. David Wood.

WOOD: I think there's possibly something in this. But there is one difference between the Lobby and most other specialist journalists. We always have at Westminster a corrective – that's to say, if we get information from one side, the other side are there waiting to provide the countervailing facts. We are dealing with a Government and an Opposition, or even if we're dealing with a party, we're dealing with the leaders of the party and their rebels. So there is the constant correction if you want to get it.

KING: Sir Harold Evans on the basis of his experience at Downing Street goes further and denies that the relationship between journalists and politicians is cosy at all. On the contrary.

EVANS: When one thinks back, I wouldn't have thought that any Prime Minister in recent times has not at some stage been pretty heavily bludgeoned by the Lobby, and I think this goes for other ministers too. I don't think that this cosy relationship exists. One has only to think of some of the treatment that was meted out at various times by the political writers both to Macmillan and to Wilson, who were of totally different complexions of course.

KING: The relationships between politicians and journalists in general may not be cosy, but of course there may be particularly close links between individual politicians and individual journalists. One charge levelled against the Lobby is that too many of its members have too narrow a range of political contacts – that when a story breaks they tend to ring up the same half-dozen or so M.P.s. John Whale remarks:

WHALE: Lobby correspondents can't have a very wide range of sources, partly because they haven't very much time, and also because they haven't very much freedom of movement.

KING: David Wood maintained that before writing a story he talked to as many people as he had time for. 'Suppose', I asked him, 'you are confronted with a story like Roy Jenkins's resignation as Labour's Deputy Leader. How many people will you try to get in touch with before you write the story for the following morning?'

WOOD: It varies enormously. It depends whereabouts the event is on the clock on the day. If it happened immediately before an edition, quite clearly you would have to use your background knowledge. And if you've lived in the place for a long period of years your background knowledge would be pretty well on the mark. If it happened three, four, five hours before you had an edition, well, clearly then you can go round and see an awful lot of people. But even if you write it rapidly for the first edition you still have plenty of time to work on it and see people before your following edition.

KING: I put it to William Deedes: 'It's said that most lobby correspondents are overtly dependent on a limited number of sources and that they often base their stories on the slenderest of foundations: is that true in your experience?'

DEEDES: I don't think that's altogether fair. My impression is that Lobby men go to great pains to check certainly the important stories that are going to make an impact, from as many sources as they can, and for this reason: your existence as a lobby correspondent, and your success in the job, depend very much on the goodwill and the trust which you engender from people who know who you are. And bear in mind that you've no alternative source of information. If you go and offend a minister with an inaccurate story, or if you go and let a Member of Parliament down, all you are really doing is to cut off your nose in order to spite your face.

KING: There is an additional problem. After any gathering of politicians that's supposed to be private and confidential, most of the politicians who were present, since the meeting was confidential, won't talk; but a few will, and they're always the same few. The politicians who don't talk complain that what we read in the papers is almost invariably the version the Lobby picks up from this talkative and unrepresentative minority. And, of course, the few who do leak things to the press almost always do so for their own purposes.

Another charge levelled against lobby correspondents is that they're not experts. Let's suppose that a particular lobby correspondent *does* know a wide range of people in both political parties, does *not* censor his own copy for fear of offending his sources, *is* careful with how he uses non-attributable material: isn't there still the problem that he's not an expert, not a specialist? Either, it's said, the lobby correspondents should work as a team with other specialists, on education, defence, and so on; or newspapers should have, not one or two men in the Lobby as at present, but maybe five or six. Gerald Kaufman remarked about the Lobby system as he saw it when he worked for the Labour Party:

KAUFMAN: I think that it worked very well for what it was meant to be, namely, a source for providing information and documents to a group of political correspondents based on the House of Commons. On the other hand, I thought that the whole system was extremely unfair to those correspondents, not because of what was done by the briefers, but because of the way their editors conceived their role. It really is absolutely absurd to expect one or two or three men to be able to cover a Vehicle and General Report, and a Rhodesia Report, and all these other things. They need much bigger staffs in my opinion.

KING: Do the correspondents, the specialist correspondents, and the Lobby people need to work much more as a team in your view?

KAUFMAN: I think that what they need is what American newspapers have, that is, a bureau. I think each newspaper needs a Westminster bureau with a political editor in charge and a large team with time and scope to deal with the extraordinary outflow of information and documents which comes from the Government and the House of Commons.

KING: For John Whale, the major single difficulty about the Lobby is that the men in it have to be generalists.

WHALE: The difficulty that Lobby men have is that they're tied to a single source. This is true, of course, of a lot of specialist journalists – environment specialists, defence specialists – they need, crudely put, to keep the favour of the department that they write about if that department is to continue to supply them with information. But they have at least some expert knowledge to weigh what they get from the department against. Now Lobby men are just as much one-department journalists; they are in fact Downing Street correspondents. But they are not specialists; they have to cover the entire field of politics, the entire field of human life, they can't possibly know enough of the detail of legislation, of Government planning, in order to check what is handed out to them from Downing Street.

KING: David Wood, however, who writes on an extraordinary variety of subjects for *The Times*, insists that what some see as a major defect in the Lobby is, in fact, its greatest virtue.

WOOD: The perfect Lobby for me would be a Lobby of which I was the only member. I think this is true of everybody – I certainly speak for the Fleet Street group anyway – and for many of the provincial men. The whole point of the Lobby, I think, is that you try to do it on your own. Quite clearly the burden is enormous, the range of political subjects these days, not only national, but international, is so enormous that you would need the Archangel Gabriel at God knows what salary to do the job properly. Nobody I would say can do the job properly. You have to be content with twenty-four hours a day, and seven days a week, and hope that you come as near as you possibly can within your own lights, not to perfection, but to an approximation to perfection.

KING: Of course, Lobby journalists aren't the only journalists writing about politics. Their position may be a central one but they don't have a monopoly – a point Sir Harold Evans was anxious to make.

EVANS: Really one must bear in mind that the Lobby is only one of many channels as between government and the press. After all, most of the essential and basic information about Government activities is given in the House itself. There are speeches in the House, statements in the House, answers in the House. There are speeches outside the House, press notices, press conferences, White Papers – everything you can think of. There are many channels; therefore the Lobby is just one channel.

KING: None the less, the Lobby is the main source for most of us of general news about politics. One still wants to know whether what the Lobby journalists tell us is true, and whether the picture they paint is a full one. Let's give the last word to William Deedes who, when he was Minister in Charge of Government Information, might well have formed a very jaundiced view of the work of his former colleages. But he didn't . . .

DEEDES: When I was a lobby correspondent, I imagined that there were a tremendous number of stories that I ought to get and didn't know about. When I was a minister in the Cabinet and had some responsibility for giving out the news, it never seemed to me possible that anything the Cabinet was doing or about to do could conceivably remain secret for more than about twelve hours. And in my view it very rarely did. But that's what different points of view will do for you. Basically, what gets out and what gets printed is extraordinarily accurate. And I think it is fair to say that the product of the system – warts and all, and there are warts – is to give the public an accurate picture of what is likely to happen in politics, and of why some other things are happening.

KING: In other words, we may not live in the best of all possible worlds as far as political reporting is concerned, but the second best we have is, I suspect, probably not too far off the best we're ever likely to get.

7 The Art of the Political Interviewer

This programme in the 'Talking Politics' series is actually more about talking than about politics. We are going to spend some time considering that new twentieth-century art form: the political interview on radio or television. We aren't going quite to turn the tables on political interviewers – we haven't invited politicians into the studio to interview the interviewers – but to discuss the art we have with us three very experienced practitioners: George Ffitch, who appears regularly on Independent Television as well as being Deputy Editor of *The Economist*; Ian Trethowan, a political journalist who presented programmes on television before becoming Managing Director of Radio in the B.B.C.; and Robin Day.

One of the things we are going to do is put to them some of the complaints one often hears about the interviewer from the general public. But, first, the question of what the interviewer is actually trying to do. George Ffitch, when you are about to interview a particular politician, or a group of politicians, how far do you think out in advance exactly what it is you want to achieve in the interview?

FFITCH: Well, the basic point of any interview – and this is true all the time – is to impart information. So obviously what you are trying to do is to impart the information of the moment. If you are interviewing Harold Wilson, for example, after the Common Market debate in the Labour Party you ask him about his attitude towards the Common Market, and to try to get over to the public all aspects of his attitude. You don't think in terms of what effect this will have on the body politic or democracy, but you do think: 'If he answers this question this way, then I'll ask this question and that.' And you are not trying to make him

Discussion broadcast on 15 January 1972.

look a fool, you are not trying to challenge him, you are not trying to usurp the role of the politician. You are simply trying to impart all available information which you can get from this politician to the viewer.

KING: Robin Day, do you ever say to yourself: 'In part of the interview I am going to let the politician state his case and use my questions just to draw him out, and then in a later part of the interview I'm really going to try to show up the flaws in that case'?

DAY: No, I don't say that, because I know that all the politicians I am likely to interview are perfectly capable of stating their case, and the problem is not whether they'll be able to state their case but whether I'll be able to get a word in edgeways on behalf of the viewer. Just to answer your first question from my point of view, of course you take an immense amount of thought – at least I do – in preparing for an interview – as to what questions you are going to ask. I had a brief period at the Bar and one of the lessons I learned there was that you don't ask a question unless you know the answer. And, therefore, in asking anybody a question in politics, having put it in your mind, you then try to find out what he is likely to answer to it. So you thereby better qualified to ask the next question, which is the one that counts.

KING: Have you ever asked yourself, Ian Trethowan, exactly what it was you were after, so that you would know at the end whether you'd succeeded in your object?

TRETHOWAN: I think one approaches every interview in a different way. When I used to do interviewing, clearly there was a great deal of difference between interviewing a current politician – a minister or a shadow minister – about some controversial issue in politics, and interviewing, say, a retired politician. I did two very long interviews with Harold Macmillan some years after his retirement about his memoirs, and clearly one aproached that in a very different way.

KING: I think one of the problems all of us have is realising that sometimes we ask questions to which we know the answers, but which we feel we ought to put on the listener's or the viewer's behalf. George Ffitch, do you ever have any difficulty with this, asking these apparently rather silly, naïve questions?

FFITCH: No. I think you do remember most of the time to say:

'Well, what does the viewer want to know?' This is coming back to imparting information. You do know that, when a politician comes into a television studio, he has come in there because he thinks it's going to do him some good. He never comes in when you want him to come in because you feel that there is a public duty for him to come in to explain his case. He only comes in when he thinks he's on a good wicket or he thinks he's forced to. So, inevitably, you ask tough questions because people expect you to ask tough questions, because otherwise you would give the man an easy wicket. You'd be doing a Party Political Broadcast for him. I think it is important to remember that television cannot force any politician to come into the studio.

TRETHOWAN: Yes, this is almost always true. There are occasions though, are there not, when a politician would ideally prefer not to be interviewed on television or radio, but feels that it is necessary for him to do so in order that he should keep himself in front of the public? – although he knows that he is bound to be asked some embarrassing questions.

DAY: I'm not sure that I agree with George about his use of the word 'tough' question. This is a common word used in the press. Of course, George is primarily a newspaperman now. In my experience, the toughness or softness of a question depends not on the question but on the answer. I have asked questions which I have taken hours to prepare, which I thought would get to the heart of the matter and put the politician in a position where he had to give an interesting answer. And I've found that he's been able to push it aside very easily. On the other hand, I've asked a question, and it had never crossed my mind that this was an objectionable question, and the chap blows up. And then people say that was a tough interview.

TRETHOWAN: But isn't toughness in the ear of the listener or in the ear of the viewer? I mean I've had occasions over the last year or two where I've had – about the same interview – a letter from some listener saying: 'But really, how dare your interviewer ask these rude and vigorous questions?'

DAY: Wasn't one of mine, was it?

TRETHOWAN: I'm sure it wasn't, Robin. And on the same interview somebody else will write in and say: 'If you are going to interview Mr X will you please get somebody to interview him who knows about the subject and doesn't ask these soft questions?'

It depends very much, I think, on the political attitude of the listener.

FFITCH: Yes. But just on this point, because of the number of people watching on television, you have more courage to ask direct questions than you would have face to face with just the two of you, which is how the newspaper journalist works.

TRETHOWAN: Could I just take up this point about the rudeness? I think this is very important. It's a question really of the interviewer being seen to play the ball, not the man. I think we'd all agree that what is bad is when the public is put in the position of being able to say: 'Who does this young man think he is, asking these impertinent questions of Mr So and So?' And, more important, the interviewee can swerve away from the point of the question and deal with the manner of the question or even the manner of the questioner.

KING: Let me put this to you. Should an interviewer ever ask a politician a question which he knows the politician can't possibly answer? One often sees on television and on radio a politician being asked, does he want to be leader of his party, or is he going to resign – that sort of thing.

FFITCH: Well, to be perfectly truthful, you have to say yes, that we do ask this. I mean, for example, at the Labour Party conference recently both Robin and myself interviewed Roy Jenkins. We asked Roy Jenkins if he was going to resign if the Parliamentary Labour Party decided to oppose joining the Common Market. Now we knew he would not answer that question. That is the sort of question which you ask because you know that the people both who you are working for in the programme and you hope the viewers expect you to ask. And if you don't ask it then they say: 'Why didn't he ask him if he was going to resign?' So there are a number of questions which you do ask, even though you know you are not going to get a reply.

DAY: And you are also interested in finding out how he answers the difficult question.

FFITCH: The Roy Jenkins interview is a very good example of this, because I sat and thought for about an hour and a half what I was going to ask him in a seven-minute interview at the end of the day on the Common Market debate, and I prepared this very carefully. Then, when he actually starts to answer it in an entirely different way to what I thought he was going to answer it, it becomes a much more interesting interview as far as you are concerned, but a very much more worrying one because you don't really know how it's come over at all.

KING: That does raise the general question of how far one decides in advance in detail exactly what one is going to ask a person and ploughs on regardless, and how far one adapts oneself to the situation.

DAY: One does both if one is any good. What one does is prepare very carefully. A short interview off the cuff is a different thing but, if one is preparing a serious interview with a political leader at an important moment, one prepares it very carefully and one anticipates the number of possibilities which will develop. Because one doesn't quite know which point he is going to reply on.

FFITCH: I think anyone who goes into a television studio, be he interviewer or politician, who hasn't thought very carefully of what he is going to be asked or what the answers are going to be, is an idiot. Because I think we've all of us seen even the most experienced politician dry up. You can see their eyes go blank sometimes and you help them out by coming in with a question. And you've all seen the interviewer who has also gone blank – and it's happened to oneself – then suddenly you think: 'Oh my God, if the man finishes his answer now I don't know what to ask next.' If you've prepared it very carefully, you can at least look down and ask some intelligent question which you've got there. It's a great aid.

DAY: I'm bound to say the major problem is not drying up, but how to get in all the stuff one has in the time.

KING: What about the situation in which the interviewer is turned on by the interviewee? I think we can all think of a couple of instances of politicians who quite like doing this, and we've probably all had the experience. And the question really is how one ought to react when this happens. One of the most celebrated instances ever of a politician turning on the interviewer was during the Profumo crisis back in 1963. As I recall, the first interview granted by any member of the Government to any broadcasting organisation was given after the crisis broke by Lord Hailsham in the *Gallery* programme to Robert McKenzie:

MCKENZIE: Now it's been said repeatedly that the leaders of the Government knew that the intelligence services were following

Mr Profumo at the time that he made his statement denying all. Now that has been repeated again tonight, for example, by the Editor of the *Sunday Telegraph* on 'This Week'. Now in this situation surely we have a right to doubt the judgement of the head of the Government.

HAILSHAM: You have a right, and the House of Commons will have a right to demand the facts, but to prejudge the facts you have no right.

MCKENZIE: But wasn't there some gullibility on the part of the ministers who saw him and couldn't get any nearer the truth than they did?

HAILSHAM: Well, that depends on how conceited you are. They included two Law Officers of the Crown, they included the Chief Whip who is a studier of man, they included the Leader of the House of Commons. They must, of course, be judged by the House of Commons. But if I were you, young McKenzie, I shouldn't make up your mind before you've heard the facts.

MCKENZIE: On the security side, Lord Hailsham, can we really say there was no security problem here, or accept any such judgement, when we do know the simple fact that the War Minister was sharing a girl friend with a Soviet agent?

HAILSHAM: Of course there is a security problem. Don't be so silly. A Secretary of State for War can't have a woman shared with a spy – if he was a spy – without giving rise to a security risk. The question is not whether there was a security risk, but whether there was an actual breach of security. Be sensible.

KING: Ian Trethowan, how would you have reacted to that situation?

TRETHOWAN: I'm sure not as well as Bob McKenzie.

FFITCH: I think that Lord Hailsham's illustration there was a case where the Government felt that they had to go on to say something and I think he deliberately went on to turn up the temperature and do it that way. I think sometimes it is very much planned.

KING: Of course it can come on the other way round. Another way that we've probably all experienced, in which a politician can try to deal with a situation, is to disarm the interviewer by getting cosily familiar with him. Here is a bit from Robin Day and Harold Wilson in 1965.

DAY: Prime Minister, may we move on to ask you (Yes) one

or two questions about defence and foreign policy? Have you not had to revise your thinking on defence, in particular with regard to the nuclear deterrent?

WILSON: No. I've many times discussed this with you here, Robin, if I may say so, in this very corner of the studio before the election. The situation is, of course – as I made clear – is that the Polaris programme has now gone too far to scrap, too far to turn back or to convert into other types of submarine.

DAY: Well, if I may say so in this building, that is what is well known as the 'family doctor technique', and I don't see any objection to it.

KING: Let me ask you whether you think that a politician coming into a broadcasting studio has a right not to be asked questions which he hasn't been warned about in advance?

FFITCH: Oh no. He ought to be good enough, goodness me, especially if he's a Cabinet minister or has been a Cabinet minister; he ought to know what the game is all about, he ought to know what he is doing and what his party's policies are, what his Government's policies are. It's perfectly fair to say 'We are going to question you this evening on this area', but to ask for specific questions to be put to him beforehand!? There are politicians who try to do this. One of the classic examples of all was Duncan Sandys in the last Tory Government, who not only wanted to know what you were going to ask, but if he didn't like the way he'd answered the questions – especially when he was doing it on film – he used to say 'Cut' and do it again.

DAY: I've never known either Mr Heath or Mr Wilson – to mention only two of them from a number of leading politicians about whom the same could be said – I've never known either of them ask for questions in advance, or to complain about questions which had been put to them afterwards. Certainly not in my case.

TRETHOWAN: Surely every politician worth his salt, when he goes into a television studio or radio studio to be interviewed, has a pretty good idea of what he is going to be asked, and what he is going to say about them or not say about them. I mean you can give only two possible exceptions: one is, I suppose, that there might be an area of sensitivity in certain foreign negotiations; and the other – again it's a very small area – is if you are going to ask a man a technical question which involves producing a lot of figures. Well, that might be a case for saying 'We are going to ask you about so and so' in advance. But otherwise I am sure that all leading politicians, when they are going to be interviewed, even if you haven't said anything to them in advance at all, they've got a pretty good idea of what nineteen out of the twenty questions will be, and they are sufficiently fleet of foot to be able to be able to deal with the twentieth.

KING: What you are saying, in effect, is that the viewer or listener shouldn't be sorry for the politician. After all, these people are in politics because they can look after themselves and one shouldn't worry too much if one sees a politician being, as it were, hounded by an interviewer.

TRETHOWAN: Well no. With great respect, I think the use of the word 'hounded' is pejorative. I think that the viewer or listener should not be given the impression of a politician being hounded, or people being rude to him, for two reasons. It's wrong, because they are major figures; also, from the interview's point of view it's counter-productive. And there is the world of difference – we come back to this question of the word 'toughness'. It depends entirely what you mean by toughness. A lot of people, hearing us talking on this programme about toughness, will have in their mind's ear – if I can put it that way – immediately the impression of rudeness. And in that sense, of course, it is wrong. But toughness in the sense that we were talking about it earlier on – and I think George Ffitch was talking about it earlier on – of asking firm, pointed questions, this is right. But there is no professional journalist worth his salt who needs to exhibit his virility by being rude to a politician.

FFITCH: I think the worst service an interviewer can do a politician is a soft interview. A politician, or anyone you are interviewing, generally takes the pace of what the interview is going to be from the interviewer. And, if an interviewer is all over the place and floundering and doesn't know his stuff, the politician doesn't look very good; perhaps he can't answer the questions that he thought were going to come up. You don't really do him a service by doing a bad interview. The bad interview is a lousy, soft, stupid interview. It is not a hard, tough, fast one.

DAY: Can I just agree with what Ian has said? Toughness is nothing to do with rudeness. I remember long ago, when George Ffitch and I were young reporters, we were about to do an interview – or one of us was – with Edith Summerskill after Aneurin Bevan had been elected Treasurer of the Labour Party. And the question we worked out to ask her – and it was George's phrasing was – 'Are you pleased, Dr Edith, that Mr Bevan has been elected Treasurer of the Labour Party?' Now this was polite, it was courteous, it wasn't tough, it wasn't soft, but my goodness she found it difficult to answer.

FFITCH: I remember it, in that caravan that we used to have in the old days.

KING: Of course, one thing politicians sometimes do is come into the studio clearly determined not to say anything at all, and one wonders indeed why they've accepted the invitation to appear. We've got one rather classic example of this – variations on the 'no comment' theme – in a recorded interview between the B.B.C. staff reporter Douglas Brown and the man who was going to become President of Malawi, Dr Hastings Banda.

BROWN: Dr Banda, what is the purpose of your visit?

BANDA: Well, I've been asked by the Secretary of State to come here.

BROWN: Have you come here to ask the Secretary of State a firm date for the act of independence?

BANDA: Can't tell you that.

BROWN: When do you hope to get independence?

BANDA: Can't tell you that.

BROWN: Dr Banda, when you get independence, are you as determined as ever to break away from the Central African Federation?

BANDA: Need you ask me that question at this stage?

BROWN: Well, this stage is as good as any other stage. Why do you ask me why I shouldn't ask you this question at this stage?

BANDA: Haven't I said enough for everybody to be convinced that I mean just that?

BROWN: Dr Banda, if you break with the Central African Federation, how will you make out economically? After all, your country isn't really a rich country.

BANDA: Don't ask me that. Leave that to me.

BROWN: Which way is your mind working?

BANDA: Which way? I won't tell you that.

BROWN: Where do you hope to get economic aid from?

BANDA: I won't tell you that.

BROWN: Are you going to tell me anything?

BANDA: Nothing.

BROWN: Are you going to tell my why you've been to Portugal?

BANDA: That's my business.

BROWN: In fact, you are going to tell me nothing at all.

BANDA: Nothing at all.

BROWN: So it would seem to be a fruitless interview.

BANDA: Well, its up to you.

BROWN: Thank you very much.

LAUGHTER

DAY: I can remember one experience like that when Lord Attlee retired as Leader of the Labour Party. 'Mr Attlee', I said to him as a young reporter, 'what title are you going to take?' 'Don't know.' 'When are you going to choose it?' 'Don't know.' 'Who would you like as Leader of the Labour Party?' 'Not a matter for me.' 'What qualities should he have, Mr Atlee?' He said: 'Sincerity, courage, intelligence.' And I had already got to the end of my postcard-full of questions.

KING: Of course, that's exactly what he was like in private conversations, too.

TRETHOWAN: Too true. I think the interesting thing about the interview with Hastings Banda was that Douglas Brown kept his cool, handled it very well. It does underline that there is really no substitute in political interviewing for sheer professional journalism.

FFITCH: No, but I wonder. I think Douglas would have been sweating like nobody's business if he'd been doing 'This Week' with Hastings Banda, and you had twenty-six minutes to fill live in the studio, and the man was going to be like that. It's all very well to do these things on tapes, but if you are doing it live, what a ghastly situation he would have been in there.

KING: What about another problem? Are interviewers inhibited by the fact that, unlike members of the general public, they, in a sense, have to live with the people they interview? In most cases they come into contact with them week after week, month after month.

DAY: These men are grown-up men, they are parliamentarians, they've been twenty, twenty-five years in the House of Commons. And anything they have to put up with in the television or radio studio is peanuts compared to what they have to put up with in the House of Commons when a mob opposite them is baying at them.

FFITCH: Well, of course, interviewing politicians on television is an incestuous business. It's almost as incestuous as this programme in many ways. But I don't think that this is the question really. You ask about members of the public. I've done a number of these programmes – with, for example, the B.M.A. questioning the Minister of Health. And they were what we call 'clients'-room tigers'. You know, at Television House, in the hospitality room there before the programme, they said: 'Let me get at him, let me get at him.' And when you got to the studio it was 'Oh Minister' and it was so polite, and they asked three questions in one, and Kenneth Robinson chose which question he was going to answer, and it was a total flop.

TRETHOWAN: It's not so much a question of being incestuous. The atmosphere is artificial. The only problem I used to find – maybe this is lack of professionalism, I don't know – I used to find it difficult to interview people whom I knew and liked very much, knew very well, because the atmosphere is so artificial . . .

DAY: I don't find this at all.

TRETHOWAN: . . . and you've got your nose powdered, and that sort of thing.

DAY: I don't find this at all. I've met the Prime Minister and Mr Wilson many times, apart from interviews. I don't know them well as personal friends, but we know one another. If I am interviewing Mr Heath, say, about the question of Northern Ireland and the loss of life there and the internment, there is no question about finding it difficult to put those questions or difficulty in putting what some people may consider to be tough questions, because it's one's duty to put them.

KING: One thing we haven't talked about at all is the *impact* of political interviewing, especially on television. After all, fifty years ago there was simply no question of this happening at all. Somebody like Lloyd George went through practically the whole of his political career without being interviewed on the radio and certainly not on television. George Ffitch, how do you think that it's mattered to British politics that this new art form, this new technique, has been introduced?

FFITCH: I don't think it's changed very much. I think you used the right word, the impact. I think that television has a great deal of *impact*; I don't think it has a great deal of *influence.* No one knows, but my guess is that it doesn't. I think that when you see a man being interviewed on television – Mr Wilson, Mr Heath, Sir Alec Douglas-Home, anybody like this – if you see them being interviewed for five minutes or ten minutes, they come over basically as you would expect to find them if you'd met them in private for five minutes or ten minutes. Now I think the terrifying thing about television is that, left to itself, it doesn't build up a character portrait of those politicians – that all these five minutes and ten minutes and half-hours do not over the years add up to a character portrait. They seem to start afresh with every television programme. I think this is the great weakness of television. We had great criticisms from people in the Tory Party about how television dealt with Sir Alec Douglas-Home when he was Prime Minister. And they used to say: 'This is not the Sir Alec that we have known for very many years.' But it was in fact the Sir Alec that they would have met for five minutes or half an hour. And he never built up as a character.

DAY: Personally I think Sir Alec Douglas-Home was not an unsuccessful politician on television. In fact, in the one election he fought as Prime Minister he came within four seats of winning and that was a damn sight closer than anybody thought.

KING: Robin Day, let me ask you a general question. Let's suppose that all of us in this room, all political interviewers on radio and television, were simply to go out of business. We were banned in some way. What difference would it make?

DAY: Well, I hope that this won't happen until Parliament is televised, because otherwise there will be a great gap in the nation's democratic communications. But, even if Parliament is televised, I think there will be a scope for people, there will be recesses, there'll be issues which aren't dealt with by Parliament, there'll be longer looks at things, and I think that we will still have a function. I don't think that television or radio interviewers are vitally important, but I think they are a useful branch of journalism and a useful adjunct to democratic communication.

KING: A final word from Ian Trethowan.

TRETHOWAN: I was just going to say, coming back to your original question, I would have thought it was beyond dispute that political interviews on television and to some extent on radio, particularly on television, do have an impact on the audience, on the electors. I think this is undeniable. How lasting it is, the impact – this is George Ffitch's point – how lasting each interview is, this is another matter. But clearly the influence of political interviewing would be less – coming back to Robin's point – if Parliament were televised, and if the politicians were seen, as it were, in their natural, central, democratic habitat, televised or, to begin with, on radio.

FFITCH: But Ian, the one thing that we do do is make politicians more interesting than they would otherwise be.

DAY: That, if I may say so, is the most arrogant statement in the entire programme.

KING: George Ffitch, Robin Day, Ian Trethowan, thank you very much indeed.

8 Whips and Whipping

In this programme we are going to talk about an unpopular group of men – a group of men who believe that what they do is seriously misunderstood by the public at large and even by some of their own colleagues – the two dozen or so party Whips in the House of Commons. We are going to look at them both as they seem to themselves – we talked to the Chief Whips of both of the major parties – and as they seem to those they whip – we talked to two backbench M.P.s who on occasion have defied their parties.

One says 'defy', but maybe defiance is too strong a word. Certainly, one of the M.P.s we spoke to, William Hamilton, the Labour Member for West Fife, made it all sound rather easy. He recalled that on one occasion, when Labour was in power, he deliberately disobeyed a three-line whip. We asked him what happened.

HAMILTON: I was sent a very stern letter from the Chief Whip, who was then John Silkin, and I was then the Vice-Chairman of the Parliamentary Party, and I sent an equally forthright letter back. He said: 'Oh, we are going to subject you to some discipline. You will stay away, you will be compelled to stay away from group meetings.' I got this letter on the Friday. I was determined to attend and did attend a group meeting on the Monday, and nothing further took place. I said 'Go to hell,' in effect, to John Silkin. And nothing else happened.

KING: And you never actually saw him?

HAMILTON: No, no. No, no. He sent me a letter and I sent him a letter and that was the end of it.

KING: What's happened on other occasions when you've rebelled?

Documentary broadcast on 2 September 1972.

HAMILTON: Nothing very much. I got a letter just a few weeks ago. I missed two votes and got a letter from the Deputy Chief Whip, and I told him in effect to get stuffed.

KING: We'll be looking in more detail at the whole business of discipline later in the programme. But in fact party discipline, although the main thing the Whips are concerned with, isn't the only thing. Francis Pym, for example, who as Government Chief Whip got the European Communities Bill safely through the House of Commons, described himself as a 'principal political adviser' to the Prime Minister. Part of the Government Chief Whip's job in this connection is to convey the views of Conservative backbenchers to the Prime Minister and the Cabinet. How does he go about collecting the opinions of his backbench colleagues?

PYM: If the Whips' Office is working right, between us all – and there are fourteen of us – we are in touch with all Members of Parliament and all party committees and quite a lot of groups of Members who form themselves into dining clubs and so forth, and between us all, we meet every day, we have our hands on the pulse of what the party is thinking.

KING: Do you make a point of actually going out and soliciting the views of M.P.s?

PYM: Sometimes I do. But I'm about the House in the evening myself, I dine there, I'm in the Smoking Room, in the corridors, talking to people all the time. And, if there is some particularly difficult matter, people will be anxious to express their views to one. One might occasionally seek their opinion on a particular matter. But the point about the House of Commons is that it is a continuous dialogue between all its Members, and we hear constantly what the views are and have to make judgements about them.

KING: More generally, the Chief Whip has to try to ensure that the Cabinet doesn't get too far out of touch with their backbench supporters, and that their backbench supporters don't get too far out of touch with the Cabinet. In Francis Pym's words:

PYM: It is a two-way linkage. The leadership and the backbenchers have got to be in sympathy with each other; therefore it is very important that each knows what the other is thinking and contemplating doing.

KING: How far in fact are you responsible in any sense for selling Government policy to the backbenchers?

PYM: Well, I think very often we are able to help explain why a certain thing has been done – very much so – and explaining that to the party, and they may feel that that is done for a good reason or they may not. But, if they feel it's been done for a bad reason or they don't like it, that is, of course, an important factor. But we can – I don't think 'sell' is the right word – but I think we can do a lot by way of explanation.

KING: By his own account, Labour's Chief Whip, Bob Mellish, plays a very similar role on the Opposition side, and plays it well.

MELLISH: I think I'm pretty good at that – that's a real pat on the back for myself – because, having been here so long and being very fond of the Labour Party and being part of it so much, I think that is one of my biggest jobs. I mix around in the Tea Room, in the bars, in the Library. I talk to my people all the time. I know exactly what they are saying. I know what their difficulties are. My ten Whips operate in a similar way. So that each day we have a Whips' meeting, and I know if there are any repercussions from some of my own people – I know about this.

KING: Bob Mellish is often credited, when he was Chief Whip on the Government side, with having helped stop the introduction of Labour's proposed Industrial Relations Bill in 1969. The story goes that Mr Mellish went to the Labour Cabinet and told them that Labour backbenchers simply wouldn't wear it. I put it to him point-blank: 'Is the story true?'

MELLISH: Ah, that's a disclosure of Cabinet. Now that's a very fair question, but I can't answer it like that. All I know is that I took over the job as the Government Chief Whip at a time when our fortunes were pretty low. And of course I understand and know the feelings of my own people here, and I certainly conveyed that to my leadership who responded. But I don't want to put any emphasis at all on any individual part I played. I think that story is now right under the bridge.

KING: It's not widely known that the Government Chief Whip, although not formally a member of the Cabinet, has for some years now regularly attended Cabinet meetings. I asked Francis Pym whether he participated fully in Cabinet discussions, or whether he contributed simply on party matters.

PYM: No, I don't participate fully because I am not a member of the Cabinet. But on party matters, on House of Commons matters, on judgements of the political wisdom of a course or otherwise, or the degree of acceptability of a proposal, I would put my view to the Cabinet if they wanted to have a House of Commons assessment.

KING: The term Whip is derived from the hunting term 'whipper-in'. The whipper-in was a huntsman's assistant who kept the hounds from straying by driving them back into the pack with a whip. As used in politics today, the term has two distinct meanings. It refers to the people, to the Whips themselves; but it also refers to the document that each Chief Whip sends out weekly to his party supporters in the House of Commons. The weekly whip sets out the parliamentary business for the following week and indicates to the M.P. how important his party rates the various items. On particularly important items the whip will say something like: 'A division will take place and your attendance is essential' – and this phrase will be underlined three times; hence the term 'Three-line whip'. Less important items will be underlined twice, comparatively unimportant ones only once. The Chief Whips on either side have the major say in determining what their party's whipping arrangements will be, just as they also have a major say in organising the business of the House of Commons. Francis Pym describes what happens on the Government side.

PYM: Well, the proposals for business each week are initiated in my office. I discuss them with the Leader of the House of Commons as well and put a proposition to the Opposition, and then in the succeeding day or so negotiate as to what is finally going to be announced on Thursday.

KING: For Bob Mellish as well as for Francis Pym, the question of organising the week's business and the question of what the whipping arrangements should be are bound up together.

MELLISH: Let me explain. First of all, one of the jobs I have to do each week is to negotiate with the Government on the coming week's business. Now that takes me probably two, three days of different types of negotiations and I think I'm a pretty good democrat. I recognise that Governments have to govern and I get on extremely well with my opposite number and we understand each other's problems and, if there is certain business coming up that I don't want that next week for various reasons, he will agree and remove it. Eventually we settle the business.

Now, I go to my Parliamentary Committee, which is my shadow cabinet, which are the people who are elected by the backbenchers. I tell them the business of the coming week. I also tell them how I intend to whip. For example, if it's a motion of censure against the Government, say, on housing, I'm going to put on a three-line whip – the most important whip I can impose. If the business, say, is the committee stage of the Local Government Bill, then I'll only put a two-line whip on. Now, having decided all that, I then have a meeting of all my Whips. I tell them what the next week's business is. I tell them what my whipping is. We discuss it and we send out, on the Thursday of each week, a whip, which is a notice setting out each day's business and how we're going to vote, whether it is the three-line whip summons, whether it is a two-line whip, or whether it is the least of all, the one-line whip.

And the point of all that is this: that on a three-line whip no Member, but no Member can pair – in other words pair off with one of his opposite numbers and leave the House that day – unless he gets permission of the Chief Whip himself; but on a two-line whip I delegate that responsibility to my own colleagues in the Whips' Office who do a very efficient job. And we live. We have the sort of Members who really do want to pair far more than they should and so we often, if I may use the phrase, 'clobber' them by saying, you're not going to pair that day and you'll stay here and vote, 'You've had your ration, brother,' and that's how it goes.

KING: Each Chief Whip presides over a highly elaborate communications network. At one point, while we were talking to Francis Pym at No. 12 Downing Street, the Government Chief Whip's headquarters, an important Conservative backbencher came on the line; at another, the Prime Minister's Principal Private Secretary put his head round the door. The portrait of Edward Heath, himself a former Whip, gazed down from the wall together with pictures of all of the other Chief Whips for the last hundred years or so; even Bob Mellish was there.

Each Chief Whip is assisted by something like a dozen assistant Whips, whose job it is to keep track of the M.P.s from particular geographical areas. The job of the Whips as a whole is to know everything they can about the M.P.s they're responsible for: their voting records in the House, their views on all major political subjects, even to some extent their personal habits. But Francis Pym denied categorically that, apart from their voting records, personal files are kept on Members of Parliament. It was once reported in an academic study that the Conservatives used to, at least, keep detailed files on individuals.

PYM: Well, I don't think so. I don't think my predecessors did and I certainly don't. The game moves far too quickly to worry about that: this is the thing that is difficult for people outside Parliament to understand.

KING: Bob Mellish, likewise, denied that he keeps files. It's part of his job to know his troops individually as far as he can. I asked him: 'How much of this information do you carry around in your head and how much of it do you file in some way?'

MELLISH: No. I don't have files. No. I, really, genuinely do carry it around in my head. We have, of course, the division records of everybody here. This is taken as automatic, that people do, in fact, have their votes recorded; but I, I don't use that for any malicious purpose. And I know my people, I know them very well and, when you've been doing the job as I have for twenty-odd years, you know, it becomes quite easy, really. I lark about with them and we laugh and we chivvy, we row, we quarrel, I have political rows all day. I reckon to do about seventy hours a week in this House, you know, and in that time they see a great deal of me and my door, of course, is always open to them.

KING: Not surprisingly, since the Chief Whip knows more about the individual members of his party than anybody else in the House, or certainly at least as much, Chief Whips have always been consulted about appointments to the Government. As Francis Pym put it:

PYM: I don't think any Prime Minister would make appointments without consulting his Chief Whip and without giving weight to whatever advice the Chief Whip gave. Of course, appointments are the Prime Minister's own in the end and he may wish to take a variety of views, but he would certainly consult his Chief Whip.

KING: Is there, in fact, a sanction that can operate here? A potential rebel might be deterred from rebelling if he knew that the Chief Whip was going to be the person talking to the P.M.

about a possible job for him in the Government at some time in the future.

PYM: I'm doubtful. I'm doubtful. Very often a rebel becomes appointed because he's a good chap in his own right and he disagreed for a perfectly legitimate reason. I don't think, really, that's a fair consideration. It may be something of a sanction; but there are many other sanctions applying to a Member quite apart from that one.

KING: And this, of course, brings us to the central question of the role of the Whips in enforcing party discipline. Most of the books on British government tell us that the Whips have enormous power. Not only can they refuse to recommend rebellious M.P.s for promotion: they can have them expelled, at least from their parliamentary party if not from Parliament itself; they can prevent Members going on parliamentary delegations; they can get them into trouble with their local associations; they can certainly shout at them.

And there's some element of truth in this picture, undoubtedly. But all of the people we talked to – both Chief Whips, the two M.P.s, and others – were emphatic that, when all is said and done, the powers of the Whips don't amount to much more than the power to persuade. I had a long talk with Bob Mellish on this point. 'Suppose,' I said, 'suppose someone does refuse to follow a Whip, does vote against the party line, what exactly do you do next?'

MELLISH: Well, first of all I get upset and then after that I have to live with it.

KING: Do you take no action at all? If somebody abstains, do you actually do nothing at all about it?

MELLISH: Absolutely nothing. In this situation the Member will know that because of the action he has taken he is going to get publicity. There's no doubt he's going to be asked questions by his constituency. His own colleagues in the House are a bit unhappy and perturbed and he has to live with his conscience. And this is how it is, and possibly at the party meeting it might be raised as to why a certain Member did not vote. Let him get up and answer, not me.

KING: But wouldn't you actually ask to see the man, perhaps give him a dressing-down?

MELLISH: No. This is a myth. Take the Common Market. It's

the best example I can think of where we really had – and really as far as I'm concerned for the first time – abstention on any scale. Last October I did interview about fifty of my colleagues, individually, pleaded with them, cajoled, begged, urged, you name it I did it, and in the event something like eight or nine of my people abstained. Well, I couldn't do no more. I'd done all that I humanly could in a public relations sense and they knew exactly what they were doing. These are all grown-up men and women who know exactly what's going on and they really don't need a Chief Whip to push and shove them around.

KING: The idea that the Opposition really doesn't need a Chief Whip was caried to its logical conclusion in the course of our conversation by William Hamilton, the Labour M.P. who told his Whips to 'get stuffed'. I remarked: 'What you're saying in effect is that the Whips, when all is said and done, don't really have any effective sanctions they can bring to bear?'

HAMILTON: No. I think it's a non-job. I would declare them redundant, quite frankly. I think particularly the Opposition Whips, the three at the top, are probably the most grossly overpaid people in Parliament for what they do, though I think there's a case for having Government Whips because it's important for them to see that the Government gets its business through. Pym was a good example with the Common Market legislation, very important for him to literally count heads. A very worrying job. But, as far as we were concerned, so far as the Opposition was concerned, people deliberately abstained, even voted with the Government for their Common Market legislation, and discipline didn't lie with our Whips, it lies in the constituencies.

KING: The style is a little different on the Conservative side, but we found exactly the same points being made. Sir Derek Walker-Smith, the Conservative Member for East Hertfordshire, is a former Minister of Health and the former Chairman of the Conservative backbench 1922 Committee; but he's been consistently opposed to Britain's joining the European Economic Community and defied the Whips repeatedly during the spring and summer of 1972. I asked him what action, if any, the Whips had taken.

WALKER-SMITH: They have naturally discussed it with me and have wanted me to vote in accordance with the party line. That is their duty, but they have not proceeded to anything that could be called unreasonable or harsh in the disciplinary sense. They understand that I would only vote against the party whip with great reluctance and because I felt, on a particular occasion, for particular reasons, that it was my conscientious duty to do so. I certainly wouldn't do so lightly and certainly wouldn't do so without paying great regard to what they say. Indeed, Mr Macmillan, the former Prime Minister, actually renounced the whip at one stage, so it is not inconsistent with loyal party membership in the general sense.

KING: And Francis Pym, on the Conservative side, advanced views virtually identical with Bob Mellish's. He, too, pooh-poohed the idea that there were any real sanctions the Whips could bring to bear. Suppose, I put it to him, you get wind of the fact that an M.P. or a group of M.P.s is thinking of abstaining on an important division. What sort of action do you take in advance of their actually doing it?

PYM: You say 'get wind of it'. I think the Members would come and tell us. We are in constant touch with them and none of this goes on behind one's back or only very, very rarely. They'll come and say they're worried about something, and then one will talk to them about it. One may or may not be able to persuade them. One may arrange for them to see a minister, to have a meeting to discuss what can be done, and the thing will be all worked out, and, if at the end of the day they adhere to their point of view and will not support whatever it is we propose, then it won't be done to kick them in the teeth which, you know, people like to think that it is: it will be done because there is an honest difference of opinion.

KING: And what do you then do? Let's suppose a single M.P., a number of M.P.s, have abstained, as they did frequently over Europe. What does one do next?

PYM: Well, there are no sanctions in point of actual fact. There will be a difference of view, a Member or Members taking one view and the Government taking another, and that is how it will be and that is understood.

KING: But would you never actually, for example, report the M.P. to his constituency association for them to take action?

PYM: Oh, most certainly not. Most certainly not. There was a stage, last session, on the early stages of the European Bill, when some of anti-Marketeers thought that was being done but, in fact, it certainly wasn't. There was no shred of evidence ever produced that that happened, and in the Conservative Party we do not do that because the association in the constituency of each Member is an independent body not connected with me or with the parliamentary machine in any other way, and when a Member comes to the House of Commons he must be and is captain of his own ship. Nobody is going to ask him to vote against his own conscience and he's got to justify to his constituents and his supporters how he votes and that's a matter for him. It's nothing whatever to do with me.

KING: But can't you make life rather difficult for a Member of Parliament who rebels, especially if he rebels persistently: make it more difficult for him to get pairs on the evenings he wants to get them and that sort of thing?

PYM: Again, no. I wouldn't stop somebody pairing on that basis – at least, I can't imagine that I would wish to – because they've got private arrangements between Members. But in any case, what can I do? I can argue, I can discuss, I can consult, I can take him to ministers, we can go round the whole thing. But if at the end of the day he takes a different view, well that is that.

KING: That is that – though, as William Hamilton and Francis Pym both suggested, an M.P. may find himself in hot water, if not with the Whips, then with his own constituency association or party. The Whips may brook rebellion: a man's local party supporters may not, and in the end they decide whether or not an M.P. is to be re-adopted.

The life of a Whip is a strange one, as you may already have gathered: the references to seventy hours a week at the House of Commons and so on. Neither Chief Whip either speaks in the House or asks Questions, and this vow of silence is taken by all the Whips on the Government side. But Bob Mellish, for one, didn't sound too much bothered by it.

MELLISH: Now, I know the urge to ask Questions, I know the urge to make speeches. I'm a very talkative chap, as you probably gather by this interview, so I do find that a bit irksome at times, but, well, I get by with it and you live with the job that you've got, but everybody knows I can have a go if I want to.

KING: I asked Francis Pym on the same point whether these restrictions on Government Whips' freedom didn't make it a bit difficult to recruit people to the Whips' Office.

PYM: It never has, so far, been found difficult to recruit them. Certainly it is an arduous life and it has its own problems. They can't speak or put down Questions and all these kind of things. That is a great drawback. On the other hand, they are doing a most interesting job. One is in the middle of things, in the cockpit of the political struggle that goes on in Westminster, and everybody who has come into the office, I think more or less without exception, has thoroughly enjoyed it, made a lot of new friends, found it extremely interesting and there has never been a shortage – at any rate so far – of people who are prepared to give up so much time to carry out this particular work.

KING: You say 'make a lot of new friends'. Don't they also make a lot of new enemies?

PYM: Well, it isn't normally the case. No, it isn't, in fact. What new ones find when coming into the Office is that they widen their circle of friends, at any rate in the political world, because they will have responsibilities in the Whips' Office for looking after a group of Members, some of whom they will know and some of whom they will not know, and moving into areas of committee work where there will be other Members whom they haven't perhaps met before, and they will find that they will make new friends because it isn't as though there is any antagonism between the Whips' Office and the back bench. We're all on the same side. We're all trying to achieve the same thing. It simply is that without the Whips the job couldn't really very easily be done, and we are there to help everybody and to reconcile views, so far as that is possible, and it is a very civilised way of reconciling differences.

KING: Almost everybody we talked to made frequent references to the institution of pairing, the arrangement whereby an M.P. can absent himself from a vote provided, first, that he can find someone on the other side who will also stay away and, second, that his own Whips agree. William Hamilton explained that the Whips don't actually arrange pairs for him. He does it on his own.

HAMILTON: I make my own arrangements. I record them. I've got a fairly regular pair on the other side and she and I make arrangements from week to week, and our Whips almost automatically agree with this arrangement and it works reasonably well.

KING: How does one go about getting a pair on the other side?

Many Members of Parliament do have that sort of private enterprise relationship.

HAMILTON: Well, I think in the case of provincial Members it's to their mutual advantage – for instance, somebody living, say, in Scotland or travelling to and from Scotland – to get a counterpart on the other side who travels up on a Thursday night and comes back on a Monday morning. And it's done on that kind of basis. I think every Member decides for himself.

WALKER-SMITH: The Whips' Office don't assist in getting pairs for Members. In the old days there used to be a pairing book and Members simply entered their names and a Member on the opposite side wanting a pair put his name opposite that. That has not existed, though, for a good many years, and nowadays Members who want a pair, either to be away in their constituency or on some other matter, have to initiate their own action to get one on what you call a private enterprise basis.

KING: Each party in the House has a special Pairing Whip who has to keep track of these private enterprise arrangements – 'the people who have to record the pairs' as William Hamilton puts it. The Conservative Pairing Whip is Walter Clegg, the Member for North Fylde. What, I asked him, does the job involve?

CLEGG: Well, my job is to concern myself with the Government's majority, to oversee the pairing arrangements which Members make between themselves, and on certain divisions to arrange for the pairing of Government ministers away abroad on duty, and that sort of thing.

KING: Do you ever allow pairs on three-line whips?

CLEGG: Yes, we do indeed. For example, you very often get pairs on overseas visits by Members. And the Government has to see, or I have to see, that these trips are properly balanced, that there are an equal number of Government and Opposition backbenchers so that the pairs are equal.

KING: Let's suppose there was an official dinner of some importance. Would you try to achieve the same balance there?

CLEGG: Oh indeed, yes. It would have to be a dinner of some importance on a heavy three-line whip, but this makes life much more civilised for ministers and for senior Opposition people who also have commitments.

KING: On what you call a 'heavy' three-line whip, what sorts of reasons does an M.P. have to give you before you'll allow him to pair?

CLEGG: Well, it would have to be some very good reason. Perhaps illness – of course that's perhaps a separate thing in itself – there may be a family bereavement, there could be – for example, we've had quite a number in the last session of Members who have got themselves involved in a constituency change and the constituency was choosing their new Member of Parliament that night, and in such circumstances we would normally allow a Member to pair.

KING: Despite the fact that every M.P. takes it for granted, pairing might be thought to be a rather odd practice. On the face of it, M.P.s should be in their places and voting. How does Walter Clegg justify it?

CLEGG: Well, it is purely a practical thing. It is not a theory at all, but it does make life more bearable for Members in that they can get about the country, they can go overseas, they can maintain their interests outside the House which I believe are essential.

KING: But of course it's not merely pairing that needs justifying. It's the whole business of the Whips' seeking to maintain party discipline in the House, an attempt that inevitably involves the Whips in trying to persuade M.P.s to vote contrary to their own deeply held convictions. Yet both the backbenchers we talked to accepted completely that only on very rare occasions should Members not go along with the party. Sir Derek Walker-Smith has been exceedingly reluctant to rebel . . .

WALKER-SMITH: . . . because if one is a member of a party naturally one expects to vote with them on all major issues. And over the years one is able to do that in most cases. But every now and again there may arise exceptional circumstances in which the strength of one's convictions compel one to do otherwise. But one should only do it after very careful thought and consideration and after giving every thought to the possibility that one may at the end of the day be wrong. But if you think you are right then it is your duty to vote in that way, however reluctantly.

KING: Francis Pym didn't really attempt to justify party discipline. Rather, he claimed it isn't really discipline in the ordinary sense that's involved.

PYM: Nobody ever asks an M.P. to vote against his conscience,

I certainly never have. The point is that it's extremely difficult for the ordinary person outside to understand what the House of Commons is like – a collection of human beings working together for a particular end, facing another collection of individuals trying to get them out of power. Now the House of Commons quite simply will not work without a proper basis for consultation and bringing together of different points of view. Now that isn't really a disciplinary process. It's disciplinary in so far as self-discipline is concerned and understanding other people's points of view and realising that you can't get all that you want in life and you've got to give and take and arrive at a proper conclusion. So that the idea, which is so prevalent in the public mind, that discipline applies and sanctions exist and I've got some medieval instrument in the back cupboard to bring out and threaten people to do things they don't want to do, is totally and absolutely untrue.

KING: When I put the same general point to Bob Mellish on the Labour side, he replied in terms that were really very similar. 'When all is said and done,' I asked him, 'an awful lot of ordinary voters do hold the view that there is something wrong with a system in which Members of Parliament are consistently invited to vote against their consciences. They think one way, the party tells them to vote the other, and so they vote that way. How would you, to an ordinary member of the general public, try to justify that system?'

MELLISH: Well, first of all I think you must understand that this story about this enormous discipline is an absolute myth. It really isn't true. That's the first thing. Secondly, of course, all Members of Parliament in this House – yes, all of them – are in this House because they are members of a political party. I am here not because I'm Bob Mellish, although I have an outstanding majority in my constituency and I think I'm very well-known and I think reasonably popular. I know that if I stood as an Independent I probably would be lucky if I got a thousand votes. Therefore, the reason I am returned to this House is because I am the Labour candidate for Bermondsey. Now I am returned as that Member, for that party. If I can make the parallel: it's like a football team. You have to work as a team and you have one objective: there's a goal at the other end that you have to score every now and again. It's pretty difficult, you know, if you are trying to be a captain or a vice-captain of a team if you get one or two chaps turning round and suddenly running the other way and kicking in their own goal. And it's bad enough trying to organise your team – particularly if you are outnumbered, as we are, by a majority of thirty-nine – if you don't get a united effort. So I say to my chaps – on this argument I would say to the public – 'Look, be realistic about this. You voted for these various individuals because they belong to a certain political party.' Now the party itself has to justify its existence, its point of view, with the public. And I say to my colleagues: 'Look, you owe a duty to the party for the very reason that you are here because you are a a member of that party.'

KING: Not everybody would accept that the party whips are either justified in trying to impose discipline at all, or really have as little power as they claim. But two things are clear. The first is that the Whips perform many useful tasks in the House of Commons apart from discipline. The second is that in the 1970s, in so far as party discipline is maintained at all, the pressures on M.P.s come mainly, not from the Whips but, as two or three people have said on this programme, from the party activists in the constituencies. Their role in the life of a Member of Parliament would have to be explored as a separate matter.

9 Question Time in the House

Some years ago a Cabinet minister was driving in a remote part of the country with the Permanent Secretary in his department. It was a foggy night and eventually they realised they were lost. 'Where are we?', they asked a farm labourer who happened to come along the road. He looked at them, a bit puzzled. 'In a motor-car,' he said. The Permanent Secretary turned to the Cabinet minister: 'That', he commented, 'was the perfect answer to a Parliamentary Question. It was true, it was short, and it gave away no information that was not previously available.'

Question Time is one of the most famous of British parliamentary institutions. It's often been copied in other countries. It's also the source of a good deal of our political news. The Prime Minister's Questions sometimes lead to major rows in the House of Commons, and the Questions asked to other ministers can lead to important statements of Government policy. For example, the announcement a few months ago that the value of pensions was to be reviewed on a regular annual basis was made in the form of an answer to a Parliamentary Question. Yet, unless they've actually been along to watch the House of Commons at work, most people are probably pretty hazy about what Question Time is and how the system works. Why are Questions asked, who prepares the answers, why is the institution important?

In this programme we are going to try to answer these questions. What we did was to take a typical Question Time on a typical Monday afternoon. We not only watched from the Gallery, we also talked about what goes on behind the scenes with one of the ministers who was answering that day, Christopher Chataway; with several M.P.s; with a Clerk of the House of Commons; and with a number of civil servants in Mr Chataway's department.

Documentary broadcast on 19 August 1972.

Take a question more or less at random: no. 14 on the printed Order Paper. On the day we were in the House it read: 'Mr Frederick Willey, Sunderland North, to ask the Secretary of State for Trade and Industry what additional employment for men is in prospect in Sunderland.'

KING: When Question 14 was reached, the Speaker called out Mr Willey's name. Mr Willey stood up and said clearly: '14, Sir.' There was no need for him actually to restate his Question because it was there for everyone to read in the Order Paper.

At this point Mr Chataway got up from the Government front bench, placed a large ring-binder on the despatch box and simply read out his answer in the usual brisk, rather perfunctory way: '740 male jobs in the Sunderland group of Employment Exchange areas. This takes no account of jobs that may arise in the service sector.'

Mr Chataway sat down again, his binder propped on his knees. Mr Willey immediately arose again in his place and again was called by the Speaker: 'Does the Minister realise that, welcome though it is, it does little more than match continuing redundancies and closures? Is he aware that the Secretary of State for Employment shocked the Sunderland Corporation recently by refusing to discuss with it the question of high and persistent unemployment in Sunderland? In view of this would he consider discussing with Sunderland the opportunities which may arise from the new Industry Bill?'

Mr Chataway, who had been looking at his notes in his ring-binder as Mr Willey spoke, returned to the despatch box: 'I am very willing to arrange any discussions which may be helpful. I am sure that the Right Honourable Gentleman has derived satisfaction from the fact that in the past two months the unemployment figure in Sunderland has dropped by nearly 1,000.'

No Member tried to catch the Speaker's eye at this point, and the Speaker called out the name of the M.P. down to ask no. 15. And so it went until, at half past three sharp, when only 31 of 77 Questions down for oral answer had been reached, the House moved on to other business. Sometimes, as in the case of Mr Willey's question, only one supplementary question was asked in addition to the main one. Sometimes there were several, with Members of both parties and occasionally Opposition front bench spokesmen intervening. Afterwards we talked to several of those who'd asked Questions and asked them why. In the case of Fred Willey the answer was fairly obvious.

WILLEY: This was a constituency Question. I am concerned about unemployment in Sunderland. I asked the same Question twelve month ago, so I was concerned about how the position had improved or got worse. In fact, I found it had got worse.

KING: Are you going to use that information for getting some publicity for the problem?

WILLEY: Yes. My supplementary question wasn't about this, because another matter had arisen meanwhile. But certainly I will use this. What I do about Questions like this is to build up a case.

KING: And when you've built up the case, the idea is that, with any luck, the Department of Trade and Industry will actually do something?

WILLEY: Oh yes. I'm not as depressed as all that about the Department. I think one of the important things about a running dialogue like this is that it very much affects the Department. I don't think that I am alone in noticing that the position has worsened. I think the Department, because they've had to answer this Question, will also notice this. They will expect me – they know me well enough – they will expect me also to follow it up.

KING: Another Labour M.P., Leslie Huckfield, asked about motor-car exhaust emission and safety standards legislation in other countries, in view of what he thought were their restrictive effects on British exports. His reasons were very similar to Mr Willey's.

HUCKFIELD: I represent, of course, a car-manufacturing constituency. Most of the people who live in Nuneaton work in Coventry, particularly in the car factories. And one of the things, I think, that is worrying the car manufacturers is the increasingly tight legislation which we find emanating from the United States on things like car safety standards and exhaust emissions. And if this, of course, is going to be detrimental to British exports, then it may well be detrimental to my constituents.

KING: And you wanted the Minister's answer to get publicity in the constituency, did you?

HUCKFIELD: Well, I want to drive home to the Minister the fact that my constituents are concerned about this and that I am concerned about this, and I don't want the Minister to get the impression that nobody cares about it, because not only the manufacturers but my constituents do.

KING: Have you asked Questions on this subject before?

HUCKFIELD: Yes. In fact this, I should say, is about the tenth Question that I've put down on rather similar subjects, so it's been a little campaign I must confess.

KING: Sydney Chapman, a Birmingham Conservative M.P., also asked about the motor-car industry, but for a slightly different reason. Why had he asked about the value of motor vehicle sales?

CHAPMAN: Genuinely because I was seeking information. Some people who ask Questions know the answer already. But the reason for asking the Question was to find out if in fact car production had gone up in Birmingham.

KING: But why did you want to know that? Just out of curiosity?

CHAPMAN: Oh no, no. So that I could ask a supplementary. I wanted to know if in fact the value reflected an actual increase in the numbers that had been sold, taking into consideration inflation, and it certainly had. And also I wanted to know if the numbers that were being exported had increased.

KING: What will you do with this information now that you've got it?

CHAPMAN: Well, there are two things. The first is that I keep in the closest touch with my leading Conservative workers in the constituency. I send them a monthly newsletter, and this will be included in it, which I think will be of interest to them. And secondly I hope that the local press might pick it up.

KING: But by no means all Questions arise out of M.P.s' constituency interests. Sydney Chapman reckons that no more than 60 per cent of the ones he puts down fall into this category.

CHAPMAN: The other 40 per cent are generally environmental questions of interest to me personally. For example, a good example of this – I've been asking a series of Questions, asking what departments are doing to encourage National Tree Planting Year, which I was lucky enough to get the Government to accept.

KING: And Dr Gavin Strang, a Labour Member from Edinburgh, asked a general Question about the computer industry that had no obvious bearing on his constituency at all. Why was he concerned?

STRANG: I am interested in the computer industry. I was a member of the Select Committee on Science and Technology which produced a very substantial report on the industry, and I am maintaining my connection with the industry.

KING: And did you ask the Question because you wanted information or because you wanted to prod the Government into doing something?

STRANG: I think a bit of both on this occasion. But we are most anxious to get a comprehensive statement on the Government's policy towards the computer industry, and indeed many of the journals in the industry have been complaining about this delay. And the great thing about the Question actually was that for once I got a little bit of information – namely, that we are going to get this statement in the near future.

KING: Question Time on most days lasts for just under an hour. It takes place every weekday but Friday, although a Select Committee recently recommended that there be Questions on Fridays, too. Questions can be asked by any M.P. not in the Government. But in practice the Leader of the Opposition almost never puts down Questions, and most are asked by backbenchers; in fact it's generally thought of as a backbench occasion. Questions can be put down either for oral answer or for written answer. Answers to the written Questions are published in *Hansard*, and so are answers to Questions that are put down for oral answer but aren't actually reached. The great advantage for M.P.s of oral Questions is that they and their colleagues can put supplementaries. Given the enormous numbers of Questions asked, not every government department can be reached every day or indeed every week, and there's a published rota, so that ministers and departments can know which of them are coming up when. Christopher Chataway's department, for instance, Trade and Industry, is first for Questions every three weeks, and also comes on second occasionally.

Apart from being restricted to two oral Questions on any one day, M.P.s can ask as many Questions as they like. But, of course, not every Question that could be asked is in fact admissible. You are not allowed to ask a minister what he thinks of the weather, for instance, or what were the causes of the decline and fall of the Roman Empire. Charles Gordon, the Principal Clerk of the Table Office in the House of Commons, which deals with

Questions, emphasised just how strict the rules of order relating to Parliamentary Questions are.

GORDON: The main rule on which Questions fall down is the rule that a Question must relate to matters for which a minister is responsible. Very often a Member is interested and keenly and legitimately interested in probing some matter, but the fact nevertheless remains that that matter is not within the official responsibilities of a minister. And if that is so, and if we can convince the Member so, well, then the Question has to be turned down.

KING: And the Question mustn't have been asked before?

GORDON: That is the second main hurdle on which many of them fall: very often, purely through the fact that Members are not under the duty which we in the Table Office are of reading through every day something like twenty pages of answers to Questions, and inevitably information is given in those answers which a Member doesn't see and doesn't know about.

KING: And these two, although the main hurdles, aren't the only ones.

GORDON: Well, obviously if a Question contains blasphemous language it would be just as much out of order as the same would be appearing in a Motion. But a Question is out of order if it is ironic or contains insinuations or imputations which are not actually on the surface of the Question, or if it is trivial, vague or meaningless – I quote the rule as it's set down in Erskine May – or if it seeks for purposes of argument information about a matter of past history.

KING: Not surprisingly, the Table Office often has to tell M.P.s their Questions aren't in order. And every day the Table Office sends out a dozen or so notes to Members asking them to come along to discuss Questions they've handed in. Charles Gordon has one story to illustrate just how hard it can be to put a persistent Member off.

GORDON: It concerns a man no longer a Member of the House, and now alas dead, the late Mr Emrys Hughes, who was one of our very valued customers and used to get quite a bit of enjoyment in pitting his wits against the Table Office. I remember on one occasion shortly after he'd left office Sir Winston Churchill gave a speech in the country saying that we'd fallen behind the Russians very badly in technological matters. This aroused a lot of interest and lots of Members put Questions down about it.

Well, at that time Mr Hughes was away for a period, but when he came back he brought in a Question or two on this matter and they were all out because they had been answered before. And during my conversation with him I said: 'Mr Hughes, this matter has been so very well explored that I really don't think that even you can come up with a new Question on the subject.' So he left the office with a quizzical smile on his face, and came back five minutes later and handed me a piece of paper on which there was the Question: 'To ask the Secretary of State for Foreign Affairs what facilities exist for members of Her Majesty's Embassy in Moscow to attend evening classes at Moscow University.' That was a very good Question and was accepted.

KING: Questions can be handed in in a very rough form – handwritten on scraps of paper sometimes – and once the Table Office is satisfied they are in order they are immediately printed. It's still not entirely clear, though, who is to answer them. Every Question put down in the field of Trade and Industry, for instance, is put down formally to be answered by the Secretary of State – the minister in charge of the whole Department. But, quite apart from the burden that would be placed on the top man if he had to answer all the Questions, many of them fall directly within the fields covered by his junior ministers. Mr Chataway, for example, is in charge of regional policy. Since there are actually eight Trade and Industry ministers in the House of Commons, somebody has to see to it that the Questions are routed to the right ministers. In Trade and Industry this job is done by the Department's Parliamentary Branch, headed by Basil Bird. As Mr Bird explained, his job involves more than just seeing that Questions are directed to the right ministers.

BIRD: The first thing the Parliamentary Branch does is to allocate the Question for answer, for a draft answer that is, to not only the division of the Department that is expert on that particular subject, but the particular part of the division and even down to the individual who will be mainly concerned with the preparation of the answer. And that allocation of Questions is in itself a pretty skilled job.

KING: And when all the work on the Questions has been done in the Department, the Questions, the draft answers, the notes for supplementaries, all come back to the Parliamentary Branch.

BIRD: Because, for one thing, we have to make sure that when the Minister goes to the House he has got the answers to all the Questions he is going to answer in a folder – in effect a ring-binder – that he has his notes for supplementaries, his supporting background material, and every answer is in the right place because, as you know, when the Question is asked in the House it's merely asked by the Member calling out the number. And everybody there who has got an Order Paper can identify the actual Question. The purpose of that is to save time. This means that the Member doesn't have to read the Question out. But it also means that we have to be quite sure that the answer has the right number, which it does have, on a projecting coloured tag. And we also make sure that that answer is only in one minister's binder; otherwise you could have two ministers jostling each other at the despatch box to answer the same Question, or it may be that no minister will get up to answer the Question.

KING: The work of preparing the materials that go into those ring-binders falls mainly to civil servants. Peter le Cheminant is an Under-Secretary in the Department of Trade and Industry. I asked him: 'When a Question first arrives on your desk, what do you do with it?'

LE CHEMINANT: The routine is that the Question would arrive in the division, not specifically on my desk, and the greater part of the work will be done on it before the Question came anywhere near me. My role is really to ensure that the Question, or at least the answer, the supplementaries and the background information and so on, which are given to the Minister take account of developments which I may know about as head of the division but which my people might well not know about.

KING: The question Fred Willey asked about unemployment in Sunderland: how exactly did Mr le Cheminant and his staff go about finding the answer?

LE CHEMINANT: Our regional office made a check of its records and found out first of all how many industrial development certificates had been issued and where the plants were not yet completed, and added up from those forms, from the application forms, what the applicants had told them earlier were the number of jobs which would arise. They then modified this in the light of their own knowledge of projects which perhaps had been delayed or hadn't in fact got off the ground, and arrived at the best estimate they could make on the basis of information available to them.

KING: In the case of this particular Question, what sorts of supplementaries did you anticipate Mr Willey might ask?

LE CHEMINANT: In fact this particular one was a Question where we didn't feel we needed to produce answers to hypothetical possible questions. It's clear from experience, both of Mr Willey's earlier Questions and from those of other Members with seats in areas which are suffering from unemployment at the present time, that it would be the unemployment aspects of the situation which concerned him. And we produced for the Minister as much relevant and helpful information as we could on such matters as what had in fact been happening to unemployment in Sunderland and on Wearside generally over recent months.

KING: So civil servants go to a good deal of trouble, not merely to answer the original Question, but to try to anticipate what M.P.s will ask next. How much do civil servants speculate about M.P.s' motives in asking Questions?

LE CHEMINANT: We are all curious creatures and obviously one speculates. On the other hand, the prime task is to answer the Question as asked and speculation relates more to possible supplementaries than to the main Question itself.

KING: How do you go about guessing what sorts of supplementaries the M.P.s are likely to ask?

LE CHEMINANT: Well, I've been a civil servant now for twenty-three years. I've been involved in Parliamentary Questions to a fairly substantial extent over that time – so of course have many of my people – and one just gets a feel for these things.

KING: How much skill is actually involved in the wording of a Question? Do you ever find yourself looking at a Parliamentary Question in front of you and saying to yourself: 'That's a particularly good one'?

LE CHEMINANT: Oh certainly, yes. Again, I think Members vary. Some are very good at and very interested in parliamentary procedure. Others are very good and interested in asking Parliamentary Questions, and in the techniques of phrasing the Question to leave ministers with the minimum of freedom for manoeuvre in answering.

KING: If that's a good Question, what's a good answer? Would Mr le Cheminant agree with the Permanent Secretary lost in the fog that a good answer is one that is true, short, and gives nothing away?

LE CHEMINANT: Oh completely, yes. Indeed, I think I'd expand on that definition slightly. I think that a good parliamentary answer, or good answer to a Parliamentary Question, must first of all be something which can be spoken. This is something that newcomers to the game sometimes forget: that in fact a minister has got to stand on his feet in Parliament and utter some words, and it's as well that he has words that he won't trip over when he's giving them. Short, certainly. This is desirable in itself. Accurate, well of course. No minister could ever afford to mislead Parliament and he wouldn't wish to do so, and a good deal of time is spent in preparing Parliamentary Questions, making sure that factual information, for example, is correct. One needs to double-check the facts to make sure that they are right. As to not giving anything away – well, this obviously will depend on the Question. But there is a good deal of truth in that proposition. One must tell the truth in answering a P.Q., but one mustn't necessarily conduct a public strip-tease.

KING: It's fairly easy to see what the askers of Parliamentary Questions get out of the exercise: information, a chance to score points off ministers, publicity – especially in the local papers. They may even, with any luck, prod a minister or a department into doing something they wouldn't have done otherwise. Fred Willey clearly hopes to gain something for Sunderland. But for civil servants and ministers there's also an advantage in Question Time. It gives them a chance to put their own points across. I asked Christopher Chataway: 'Have you in your ministerial career found Question Time useful as a platform for making policy pronouncements, or at least for releasing information that you want to make public?'

CHATAWAY: Yes, yes. And quite often one thinks 'What do I actually want particularly to say today?', and then you look through the questions to see whether there is one on which you can hang something that you very much want to say.

KING: Of course, very often Questions are, from the Government's point of view, premature. They raise issues that the Government as a whole, or a particular department, hasn't yet decided on. I asked Peter le Cheminant what he and his colleagues do in this sort of case.

LE CHEMINANT: This is where the particular art of answering Parliamentary Questions comes in. One is faced with the dilemma that no minister can, or would wish, to mislead Parliament. Therefore, one has got to give as honest an answer to the Question as is possible. Certainly the answer must not under any circumstances be dishonest. On the other hand, one can face a situation where it may well be that there is a choice of options before a Government on which they haven't decided; they haven't finally made up their minds on their policy. And if one reads *Hansard* closely one can perhaps pick out the ones where chaps were ducking.

KING: If you stop and think of it, Question Time could be rigged. Suppose, for example, that Opposition M.P.s were putting down a whole spate of Questions that the Government found embarrassing; the Government might be tempted to get its own backbenchers to crowd the Order Paper with Questions of their own. The Government might even go so far as to tell its own supporters what the Questions should be. And in fact allegations of exactly this sort were recently investigated by a select committee, which has condemned any involvement on the part of civil servants in preparing Questions of this kind. But, leaving civil servants aside, I asked Christopher Chataway how widespread the practice is of ministers putting up sympathetic backbenchers to ask Questions.

CHATAWAY: Not very. It's a standard practice that, if you do have information that you want to give, maybe a statement you've got to make, you try to persuade a backbencher to put down a Question. And I think nobody objects to that. But there is a line to be drawn, obviously, and it would be very undesirable if backbenchers were persuaded to put down a whole lot of anodyne Questions simply for the benefit of the minister.

KING: M.P.s wanting to put down oral Questions are required to give two sitting days' notice. But in fact Questions often come in a week or more before they're down for answer. When the civil servants have done their work the minister begins to take an active interest. I put it to Christopher Chataway: 'The civil servants provide you with briefs for what they think are likely supplementaries: do you ever find yourself supposing that the

M.P. will actually go off on a different tack and ask them to get briefs on some other matter as well?'

CHATAWAY: Yes, very frequently. Inevitably the civil servants who are interested in their particular area assume that the Member of Parliament will ask specialist Questions about the subject that he's chosen. Very often, as a politician, one recognises that the fellow politician's intention is not to do that at all: that his Question is simply a peg on which to hang a much broader political charge.

KING: Were you taken by surprise by any of the supplementaries on Monday? I have in mind particularly Fred Willey's raising this question of whether or not the Sunderland Corporation should be allowed to see one of your colleagues, the Secretary of State for Employment. Now that presumably is something you might not know anything about.

CHATAWAY: No, I didn't know anything about it, but it is obviously the case that ministers can't see all the deputations who want to come to see them and very often, therefore, a minister writes back to a particular town and says: 'Would you talk to my regional office first?' And the Member of Parliament then says in the House of Commons: 'Disgraceful, he won't even talk to my town council' or whatever. So although I didn't know the details of that particular case, the gambit – so to speak – is a fairly familiar one.

KING: Over the years Christopher Chataway has had a lot of opportunity to observe ministers at the despatch box at Question Time. What factors does he think contribute to a minister's doing well there?

CHATAWAY: I think having a grasp of your subject is very important, and it does come out over a period, I think fairly clearly, whether a minister is simply reading out a brief or whether he really has got a grasp, because you can't ever tell quite what the supplementaries are going to be. And if the difficult supplementary is always answered with the reply 'Well, that's another question' and the minister is hesitant over any unexpected question, well, you get the impression of somebody who really hasn't got a very great deal of grasp of his department. So I think that's important. Humour counts for a great deal. And I think the third thing I'd pick on really is a willingness to take the House of Commons seriously. A minister is, I think, never successful in the House of Commons if he is really so preoccupied with his departmental issues that he can't conceal the fact that he's really rather impatient about having to answer in the House of Commons.

KING: But, still, what does it all add up to – the tens of thousands of Questions and all the work put into answering them – much of it wasted, incidentally, since so many oral Questions for which answers to supplementaries have been got ready are never actually reached. Fifteen years ago an eminent American, President Lowell of Harvard, claimed that the system provides 'a method of dragging before the House any acts or omissions by the Departments of State and of turning a searchlight upon every corner of the public service'. A bit overstated perhaps, but it's interesting to find an official, Peter le Cheminant, admitting readily that the whole exercise, far from being a nuisance, is worth the trouble.

LE CHEMINANT: I think it's well worthwhile. It's a considerable discipline on governments in general, ministers and officials, to be faced with the cross-questioning type of Question sessions which are part of our parliamentary practice and procedures.

KING: And Christopher Chataway, who has asked Questions as a backbencher as well as answered them as a minister, is of the same view.

CHATAWAY: It isn't an occasion, obviously, for detailed probing of a minister. It's fair to say that the cards are pretty heavily stacked on the minister's side. The questioner doesn't have the opportunity of following up supplementary after supplementary as a television interviewer, for example, does. You are not going, therefore, to be probed in depth. But it is an occasion on which you can give a very wide range of topics an airing. And an occasion on which weaknesses in the Government's case can be opened up.

KING: Also weaknesses in the ministers themselves.

CHATAWAY: Yes, yes. It's usually only, you know, just the opening of the door that takes place at Question Time. But it then gives to the Opposition or to a backbench Member the indication that perhaps something is wrong, and he can seek other opportunities of taking it up more fully.

KING: It's not, then, the only way that Members of Parliament can keep a check on Government, nor even the most important way. But at the very least it's a useful weapon in the armoury of weapons that M.P.s have available to them. And Question Time is important in another way: it emphasises the extent to which, in the British system, individual ministers are individually responsible for the acts of their departments. At Question Time there is, for the moment, no such thing as 'the Government' or 'the civil service'. There are only individual ministers answering, as individuals, in their own fields. They in the end are responsible. They, as the Americans say, have to carry the can.

10 Debates on the Floor

Parliament isn't *only* a talking-shop, as we've tried to show in some of the programmes in this series, but it is *at least* a talking-shop. After all, the word Parliament itself – '*Parlement*' in French – originally meant speaking or talking or conversing. And most people, when they think of Parliament, probably have mainly in mind the debates that go on there.

Well, what about them? How good are the debates in the House of Commons, how important are they? Three M.P.s generally thought to be amongst the best debaters now in the House, if not *the* best, are Sir Geoffrey Howe, who as Solicitor-General spent hours in the House of Commons in the spring and early summer defending the Government's European Communities Bill; Michael Foot, once a formidable debater from the back-benches, now Labour's shadow Leader of the House, who spent hours opposing that very same Bill; and Jeremy Thorpe, the Leader of the Liberal Party. I put it to them: when one sits in the Gallery of the House of Commons listening to debates, one very often hears M.P.s say things like 'the public is listening very closely to what we're saying tonight'. But how far, in fact, do you think people outside the House of Commons are conscious of the debates that go on inside? Geoffrey Howe.

HOWE: I think in terms of general flavour they are: in other words, they can get a broad message coming through and they can get a message coming through if an argument has gone totally well one way or totally badly the other way. I don't think one is very conscious much of the time of them listening to particular ringing phrases of particular speakers.

KING: Michael Foot, I had the experience as a university teacher once of asking, I think, some thirty first-year students of

---

Discussion broadcast on 26 August 1972.

politics what had been debated in the House of Commons the day before, when a major censure motion had been put down by the Opposition, and, in fact, not one of the thirty students could give the answer. Would you be surprised by that?

FOOT: No, I don't think I would be really. I think compared with, say, even twenty years ago the reporting in the newspapers of the House of Commons has so much declined, and so much less space is given to it, that many fewer people do know what is happening in the House of Commons. And I don't believe that the reports on television or the radio are a substitute for the extent of the newspaper reporting. If you take the popular newspapers, for example, today the amount of reporting is derisory, and that obviously has an effect. Certainly, if you compare it with the supposed days of Gladstone and Disraeli and the rest, people obviously did know what was happening in the House of Commons that week. So I do believe there has been a great change in the amount of public attention given to detailed debate.

KING: Jeremy Thorpe, as Leader of the Liberal Party, how far do you feel that the House of Commons, the debates that go on there, actually help your party put its message over in the country? Are debates important to you?

THORPE: Well, I think that the answer to that question is the same as the answer relating to the whole House of Commons. It depends on what is reported. And the outside knowledge of the House of Commons depends on what is carried in the newspapers – which, as Michael Foot says, is very little – and what is carried on radio and television. As far as a minority is concerned, if one is reported, if one has started a debate or stimulated an issue, of course it's very helpful to get across the fact that one is alive and kicking. But I think the trouble is that the public have a sensationalised view of the House of Commons largely because that is how the press report it. The press, for example, are far more likely to report in full some complaint that somebody has used six members of the Brigade of Guards to go to a garden party and query 'has public expense been involved?' or whether it's necessary to have a licence to import wart-hogs into the country than a debate which might have taken place on housing or the cost of living in which either some very damning statistics may have been put forward by the Opposition or alternatively some practical measure of alleviation may have been put forward by the Government; that is much less likely to get reported than the sensationalism or the personal attack between one person and another.

KING: But, if all three of you are conscious of the fact that you're not getting, as you think, properly reported, that the press isn't giving Parliament enough coverage, could I ask all three of you, when you get up to speak in the House of Commons, if you're fairly conscious of not speaking to the country, who are you speaking to? Geoffrey Howe.

HOWE: Well, it depends on the debate and on the occasion obviously. Primarily I think you're speaking to the House of Commons as it is then composed. It may be a very small House if it's some narrow committee debate, it may be a large set-piece occasion in which you're speaking to your own party and to the other side and through them to the outside world. You're perhaps speaking to the parliamentary correspondents, the reporters, in trying to get across through them to the public an impression. You use them as an amplifier but you start with the chaps you've got in front of you.

THORPE: Yes, I agree and I don't think one must underestimate the importance of it vis-à-vis the country. For example, a Government that habitually fails to defend itself – I'm not mentioning any particular Government, I have none in mind – but on a particular issue this inadequacy of defence will get through to their own supporters and eventually it will percolate down to their supporters in the country and this in turn will lead to a lowering of morale and this is the process whereby one Government goes out and another comes in.

HOWE: And also the place can blow up into a crisis or into a scene quite unexpectedly, not only in Question Time but also in debates themselves. You can't prophesy for certain what is going to happen any week, you can't prophesy what's going to happen any day. It's quite possible, because of the failure of a minister to defend himself, or because of the failure of somebody to do something properly, or because of some sensational attack, that the whole mood of the place can be altered very swiftly. To a great extent in my opinion, this happens more when you've got an intensive fight over a Bill in which people are generally interested and where, of course, more people are participating. It's more likely to occur, but that's why I think that the conduct of such Bills and such legislation is the most interesting part of the House of Commons. It is the cumulative effect on reputations, on morale, on postures generally, that makes the House of Commons still the centre of most political discussion.

THORPE: And it's also a very, very important safety valve.

FOOT: I agree with what Geoffrey Howe says about people's reputations and about what happens in the place. People, for example, in the House of Commons who have got a manner which may not be satisfactory or may not be appealing in many other places, because of their knowledge and because of the understanding which Members have come to have of them: people have over a period compelled the House of Commons to listen to them even though they were saying things that the bulk of the House of Commons didn't like or they found objectionable and all the rest. And so in a kind of way the place does sort out the Members that they're going to listen to. It's a very awkward thing to run an assembly where people argue and debate and where six hundred egotists are trying to deal with what's happening but each one has got the chance if he wants to force the place to listen to him in some way or other.

KING: But could one argue the reverse proposition? Could one argue that, in fact, perhaps parliamentary debates play too *large* a part in determining the reputations, particularly of ministers? Can one not think of ministers who were actually good departmental ministers, quite imaginative, who had quite a good command of the facts and so on, were doing quite a good job but, simply because of some rhetorical failure, some failure of speech-making ability in the House of Commons, didn't go as far as they should have done? Geoffrey Howe, does this ring a bell at all?

HOWE: Part of one's rational being might make one think that it ought to ring a bell. But I don't think that it does, and I don't think that it should. It re-echoes the recent complaints about how terrible it would be to choose presidents and prime ministers through television and that's merely a different presentation of the same argument. And I'm not much attracted to the proposition, for example, that it was very unfair that the democrats of Athens, as long as they were democratic, were governed by a chap called Pericles, because he happened to be a marvellous orator. If that's the system of government that we have got, and it seems to be as good as any that we can devise, it doesn't seem to me to be unreasonable to require the people who seek leadership in that kind of way of life to qualify for it in the way in which they set about it.

FOOT: Besides which, the House of Commons is not conducive to oratory. Most of the speeches that are made in the House of Commons are not orations at all, they are almost conversational. The way in which the House of Commons is organised is one which doesn't encourage people to engage in great set-piece oratory. The atmosphere is much more one which is making it essential that people should try and persuade, if they're going to succeed at all. And, therefore, many of the people whose reputations in my opinion are made in the House of Commons are not made because of what people would call oratory in an old sense; they're made because of their persuasive powers, which may not be persuasive powers elsewhere but may be in the House of Commons for the very good reason that you've got to persuade people to listen to you, that's the first thing.

KING: It's implicit in much of what you're saying that, in fact, there really are very different kinds of debates in the House of Commons, and maybe in some of them – censure debates and so on – something like oratory is a bit more appropriate than in cases where one's, for example, thinking of amending the Local Government Bill. Jeremy Thorpe, do you have a sense in your own mind that there are these distinct kinds of occasions?

THORPE: Oh, yes indeed. I think there are. I don't know how many there are because I haven't sought to categorise them, but there is certainly the occasion where a minister may be very boring, but if he is able to think lucidly and can give to the House some straightforward and candid explanation of what he has in mind and answer Questions, he will be accepted even though he may not be reaching the flights of oratory. There are then the great set-piece occasions and I must say that the great phrase, the crack, the well-turned phrase, has to be very well done because the House of Commons will react against it very, very sharply indeed. And then there are what are, I think, sometimes the most exciting debates – the ones where there is an entirely free vote and one has no idea how the vote is going to go at the end of the day: like the Hanging Bill, the Bill on abortion. I would like to see many more occassions on which there was a free vote.

KING: How far is the real debate in the House of Commons

these days – the debate that might actually influence Government policy – taking place, not in the chamber as a whole, but on Bills upstairs in standing committee, really largely away from the public gaze? Geoffrey Howe.

HOWE: I would have thought that a large proportion of the debate, about almost anything, is going on outside the chamber of the House of Commons as well as inside it. I wouldn't concentrate my attention on debates in the standing committee upstairs. I think that from time to time a real issue may emerge there and influence government. The Government is in truth being influenced by the whole mass of comment and public discussion, including quite often three well-timed Questions in Question Time as much as a whole debate.

FOOT: Every M.P. performs his parliamentary duties in a different way. None of them does it in exactly the same proportion of activities in the House of Commons and in outside committees or in party meetings and the rest. If every Member of Parliament tried to perform his function in the same way, that is, if every Member of Parliament tried to concentrate on making speeches in the debating chamber itself, well the whole thing would be jammed within a couple of days. But there is always the sanction at the end that the Member has got, that if he can't get his voice heard or what he wants to say heard either in his own party or in the committee or elsewhere or by direct application to ministers, eventually he's got the chance of coming to the House of Commons and kicking up a row there. And it's the fact that he can do that in the end which makes the whole thing work in my opinion. That's one of the reasons why I'm very much opposed to the abandonment of the forum of the House of Commons itself as the centre of the House of Commons. If you try and dissipate it through too many of these committees, then you land up in the situation they have in the United States where I think that the power of the House of Representatives or of the Senate is greatly reduced as opposed to the competing committees.

HOWE: I see the point that Michael Foot is making about the importance of the ultimate right to go to the chamber and challenge the minister there or raise your point there. But I would have thought that an extension of the range of select committees and so on would actually better equip the Member to go to the chamber in the last resort and raise the issue.

THORPE: I think it's the only forum in which you could guarantee intensive cross-examination of the minister on his policies.

KING: Somebody mentioned the need to avoid chaos in the House of Commons and clearly it's mainly up to the Speaker to do that. Jeremy Thorpe, in fact, how does the Speaker determine the order of speakers, and who will speak?

THORPE: Ah, I doubt if any Member of Parliament other than the Speaker knows and, if the Speaker knows, he'd be very unwise to say. But obviously the two front benches wish to open the debate and will make it known which minister and shadow minister they would like to open and which minister and shadow minister they would like to close. Then there are rights given to those who hold different views perhaps from their own parties or who are experienced on a particular subject. A much criticised right is that a Privy Councillor has the prior right to be called over a backbencher, and I'm in no position to criticise it because I'm a beneficiary. And there's always the right for the minority to be called. I think, for example, if you take a Northern Ireland debate, there are obviously Ulster Unionists and Nationalists and Republicans who have a very special right to be called, particularly if Stormont isn't sitting. So I think the Speaker has a very difficult job but I think that's roughly how he approaches it.

KING: Michael Foot, Jeremy Thorpe raised this question of the difference between front- and backbench speeches; there were clearly these two separate categories in his mind. You've been a distinguished backbencher, you're now a frontbencher: just how different is the kind of speech you make in these two situations?

FOOT: Well, if you're a frontbencher, you know you're going to get in, which maybe diminishes the effect of what you're going to say because it may be written off in advance to some extent. And one of the advantages of the House of Commons and the way its business operates in my opinion is that backbenchers, if they want to get in, can usually see in the next week's business the way in which they can put across what they want to say, or the next fortnight. The whole thing is extremely flexible. Sometimes in the set-piece debates this doesn't appear to be the case because there are many Members crowding to get in, and many more than the Speaker allows in, and it does appear that sometimes the Speaker has a list and the list is too orderly and is too fixed in advance. I remember one of the first occasions when I was in the House of Commons in 1945 after the 1945 election when it appeared that the Speaker had some list of speakers that he was working from. James Maxton got up and protested from the I.L.P. bench and said that he had never sent his name in to the Speaker to be called in the whole of the period he'd been a Member of Parliament and it was a scandalous thing that this practice of the Speaker having a prepared list was operating. There are prepared lists that operate now, there's not the slightest doubt, and I think it should be more flexible.

KING: But is it the case that having these lists means the debates are very often cut-and-dried, set-piece affiairs – that there isn't much actual debating?

THORPE: Certainly, as Michael Foot says, the lists exist, but my impression is that they're very flexibly used. One has an indication that the Speaker has a kind of catalogue of people whom he's likely to call. I think that it is very frustrating for a back-bench Member who's perhaps tried to speak on three successive debates on economic policy and always come out number nine on the Speaker's list for his side. And I think that the Speaker does actually try and work it more sensibly than that. But, even so, it probably still isn't used as spontaneously as one would do it if one was doing a theatrical production and wanted to pull in the next voice to come in effectively next. It's very difficult to get the right balance.

KING: What are the sorts of people whom the Speaker is going to be particularly concerned to call? You've already indicated that spokesmen for various kinds of minority interests and so on are more likely to be called, minority points of view. But are there any other kinds of people in the House?

THORPE: Oh, yes, obviously the Chairman of the 1922 Committee who is the Chairman of the Tory Party's backbench committee I'd have thought had a very good right to get in. I should have thought that if there was a debate on industrial relations the Chairman of the Labour Party's Trade Union Group obviously should be called. I think the Speaker must have some regard to the expertise of Members and perhaps the positions which they occupy – as chairman of their party's trade and industry committee or their legal panel or whatever it is. And I don't think there's anything wrong if Members say: 'I'd like to be called on this particularly because I'm chairman of such and such a committee', and then I would have thought that they had a slightly greater right to be called and I'm sure this is taken into account.

KING: Turning the whole thing the other way round, each of you has been in his time a backbencher: when you were in that capacity how did you decide what sorts of subjects you wanted to speak on? Geoffrey Howe?

HOWE: Sometimes on a subject that I was continuously and regularly and actively interested in. One was more often frustrated actually when one tried to come in on that kind of debate than on any other, because they tended to be the more popular debates, and one tended to want to make the same speech three times before one had made it, by which time it wasn't worth making. And on the other hand one found a number of occasions when you weren't expecting to have an opportunity – some topic came up late at night, or a consolidated fund debate, or something of that kind that hadn't been foreseen, which often gave one the best opportunity of making an almost unprompted contribution which was quite sensible.

KING: You mean you were just sitting there and you decided you wanted to say something?

HOWE: Yes, or one heard that it was coming up – off the programme, as it were.

FOOT: The horror of the House of Commons undoubtedly for many Members, and for new Members especially, and I remember it very well indeed, was sitting there for a whole debate having spent quite a long time preparing a speech, and preparing it for that particular moment, and then waiting till ten o'clock and discovering that you weren't going to have a chance. Now that went on several times, until at last I think that you learned the lesson that it's much better to take the risk of making a much worse speech, not having prepared it so well, and therefore not to be so disappointed if you don't get in. And, in fact, as I say, if you make up your mind to get in, there are many more occasions in which it can be done than people imagine, particularly because the House of Commons is legislating all the time, and therefore you can get in on committee stages, or report stages. So you have to adapt what you want to say to some extent to what is the programme before the House of Commons itself. Otherwise, if you just wait for the occasions when you want to say something special, well, you may wait forever.

KING: Jeremy Thorpe, these two other gentlemen have both used the phrase 'a good speech', talked about themselves or other people making good speeches, sometimes impromptu. What, in fact, in your view is a good speech in the House of Commons? What are its characteristics?

THORPE: One which 629 other people, who are egocentric and are bored listening to every speech except their own, reluctantly find they're listening to with some interest and attention.

FOOT: The House of Commons is the rudest place in the world pretty well, and, as Jeremy Thorpe quite rightly says, most of the people you're addressing are waiting for you to finish. They want to make their speeches themselves, or they think they have heard it all before. Therefore – and this doesn't only apply to the House of Commons, I think it applies to speeches generally – the most important quality in a speech is surprise, and if you can surprise yourself, as well as other people, well, that's one way of those which alter the trend of the argument, which present the achieving the result. But I believe that the best speeches are argument in a way that is different from what people have expected.

THORPE: I think Churchill once put it very cynically, but with a fair amount of truth. He said: 'In the House of Commons the first thing that matters is who you are. The next is how you deliver what you say, and the third is what you actually say.'

HOWE: But I think that something by way of response to those points might come out in the opposite direction to what Churchill was thinking. In a sense I think that the central quality of success is spontaneity and surprise, as Michael Foot was saying, and I should have thought from my comparatively limited experience on either side that it's much easier to make a good speech, and a spontaneous speech, which is the kind of speech that I like making, and I enjoy making, if you're speaking other than from a front bench. It's much easier to make a good speech if you're winding up for the front bench than opening for the front bench, because speaking from the front bench at the commencement of a debate you are required and expected to cover a certain amount of material, which is very inhibiting.

FOOT: Going back to Churchill's statement that Jeremy Thorpe quoted, of course, Churchill never, or very rarely, made a debating speech that I ever heard in the House of Commons. He may have made it in his youth much more, but, of course, Churchill had prepared it down to the last phrase. It was magnificently delivered, but it was never a speech that, or rarely a speech that, really caught you by its surprise in my opinion. Therefore he wasn't a debater in that sense, he was an orator, and he was an orator who was prepared, and the effects were all prepared. Well, that's quite different from somebody getting up immediately after a person like Churchill to reply, and that's why I think Aneurin Bevan was the best that I've seen there, because he could alter a whole speech in the course of delivering it, and you saw the whole thing turn into a different trend from what they'd expected.

KING: But could I challenge you on a point I think you all agree on? It does seem to me that the criteria you're applying for a good speech are almost theatrical. Isn't it possible that a speech that doesn't, in fact, meet any of your criteria may nevertheless have a considerable impact, while one that's a howling success, draws people into the chamber, when all is said and done may leave no mark on the course of history at all?

HOWE: Well, I think the theatrical test is a relevant one, whether you're preaching from the pulpit, or performing from the stage of the Palladium, or an advocate in court, or a lecturer, or politician, it is part of the business of persuasion, and we shouldn't shun the theatre as an element in that.

FOOT: Yes, I agree with that, but I don't think it's a matter of theatre so much. I think it's a matter of a person impressing his own personality, or his own idea, on people through the way in which he says it. And it's also a question of his gaining allegiance and support amongst his own people or causing confusion amongst the others. So I don't think there's any one way in which a speech is made. There are a whole series of different circumstances in which different speeches have to be delivered. And that's one of the interests of the House of Commons. And, although the place, I think, doesn't have as much drama in it as it used to, for a variety of reasons, I think it still is a place where you have to capture the ear of the audience in order to have a chance at all. You have to persuade, and that's a very difficult game to do. And therefore you have to apply your mind to the problem of getting into the other fellow's mind. You don't mean you're going to convert anybody by what you say, but you have to be saying something which is sufficiently persuasive to jerk him out of his torpor.

THORPE: Yes, and I would have thought that perhaps one of the most theatrical debaters of the century was probably Lloyd George; but that meant that he was able to appeal to every conceivable human emotion. At one moment it was withering scorn, but the next it was an appeal to people's sense of compassion. Next he might be appealing to the intellect with some proposition which he was putting forward. Now, I suppose you would say those are all theatrical uses of his talent, but that doesn't mean to say that one is strutting up and down like a Shakespearian actor. You're appealing to every known human emotion.

FOOT: And also the impression of a personality. Now, one person who wasn't theatrical, but who was tremendously effective in my opinion in the House of Commons, was Stafford Cripps, because Stafford Cripps had this air of authority, that anything he said – he didn't say it in brilliant English, or anything – but anything he said you thought must be true because of the authoritative manner in which he spoke. And many times I remember in the 1945 Parliament Stafford Cripps answering Churchill. He could be far more effective – I don't mean he always was, but could be far more effective – because he managed to convey the power of his personality by the way in which he spoke. Now that's not theatricality, that's the whole person making an imprint on his audience.

KING: I realise you're all interested parties in this, but, still, Geoffrey Howe, what do you think of the quality of debates in the House of Commons? Do you think the general level of style, of delivery, and more particularly of content, is high or as high as it ought to be?

HOWE: I think it's pretty high and can on occasions be remarkably high, though there are obviously occasions when it's profoundly drab. I should have thought that during our long debates on the European Communities Bill, considering the dry nature of the material which was being discussed at certain points, the debating quality of most of them was very frequently very good indeed. They were true debates, but it's not always like that.

KING: Jeremy Thorpe, would you share this view?

THORPE: Yes, I would, and I think you have to remember that the whole type of debate is different. You don't expect a two-hour speech, except perhaps on a Budget, whereas this was the thing that you would have expected in the Victorian age. One is debating important vital humdrum things, like social security and pensions and various regulations and Factories Acts, and all these sort of things, which haven't, to put it in a nutshell, got very much sex appeal – as speeches for great oratorical flights. But I think the standard basically is good. I think at times, of course, it is appallingly boring, but I think that was always the case.

KING: Michael Foot, you've been in the House of Commons longer than the two others. Do you feel that the standard of debate, however high it is now, has actually been higher at some time in the past?

FOOT: Well, I think the standard is pretty high now, but I think there are not many people who are of the top calibre that I have heard, like Aneurin Bevan or Churchill. Enoch Powell is in the same kind of standard. But there are not as many as there used to be. I know, of course, people think that it was different when they were younger, but I don't believe that's the sole explanation of it. There were a whole series of others who were extremely good individuals at it, but I believe the standard of argument and debate in the House of Commons is probably as high as – the general standard is as high as it ever was. There are fewer, say, startling individualists than there were, say, twenty years ago.

KING: Michael Foot, Jeremy Thorpe, Sir Geoffrey Howe, thank you very much.

11 A Select Committee at Work

We are going to be dealing in this programme with one of the least-publicised, least party-political, but by no means least important aspects of the work of the House of Commons: the work of select committees. It's a pity that the term 'select committee' is so off-putting. It suggests a board-room full of elderly gentlemen deliberating ponderously on some rather dreary matter, whereas, in fact, select committees often attract younger Members of the House and deal with matters of self-evident importance. Here, for instance, we are going to be looking particularly at the work done by one select committee on the subject of family planning and Britain's population.

It's also a pity that the term select committee gives one no idea of what these committees actually do. The point is that they are all-party committees set up to investigate broad fields like public expenditure, race relations and immigration, and the procedure of the House of Commons itself. What distinguishes them from most other Commons committees is that they don't just consider bills and papers. They actually summon witnesses and cross-examine them. In other words, they hold 'hearings' in the style of congressional committees in America. Later on we'll be talking to several people who've appeared before and been grilled by a select committee.

The committee we've picked out to look at closely is the Select Committee on Science and Technology. It was set up late in 1965 and has had only two Chairmen. When Labour was in power the Chairman was Arthur Palmer, the Labour Member for Bristol Central. Now it's Airey Neave, the Conservative Member for Abingdon. The Committee has enormously wide terms of reference. They say simply that 'the Committee shall consider

---

Documentary broadcast on 30 September 1972.

science and technology and report thereon from time to time'. In fact, we asked Airey Neave whether he and his colleagues didn't find such general terms of reference a bit disconcerting.

NEAVE: Well, originally, five years ago, I thought it would be rather wide to have just the terms of reference 'science and technology', and we rather went in in those days for big subjects covering a whole session of Parliament. Since then we haven't found this difficult. Of course, we can choose any topical subject we wish. And we have gone in more for the subjects which the Government are considering at the present time – the big industrial and scientific decisions.

KING: The Committee has a majority of members of the governing party on it, and the Chairman always comes from the party in power. But obviously, if the Committee is to work effectively it can't allow itself to become just another arena for the party-political battle. It must choose subjects to investigate that don't raise straight questions of party policy. And the members of the Committee have to be determined to work together pretty much on a non-party basis. I put it to Airey Neave: 'Does the Committee ever get into an area that is controversial between the parties?'

NEAVE: No, we never do this at all. In fact we have very successfully kept party politics out of science and technology, and we hope to continue to do that. We think we've got some objective people on this Committee who are really dedicated to studying the subjects in hand, and who are also equally enthusiastic about making the select committee system as such effective and making ministers and civil servants accountable to Parliament. That is the real point.

KING: Indeed, we were impressed the day we went along to watch the Committee in action by the fact that, apart from their clothes and maybe their accents, it was impossible to distinguish, in terms of the actual questions they asked and the points they made, between Labour M.P.s and Conservatives. We asked Professor David Glass, who'd given evidence, whether he could tell the difference.

GLASS: No, I think there was very little evidence of that. Much less evidence, for example, than if you look at the *Hansard* debate on the Population Statistics Act of 1938. I mean you could certainly see who the Labour Members were, you know, in the debate on whether we should have better vital statistics, for example. But, no, I thought that there was a general agreement which went beyond party lines on what questions were relevant about the future of the growth of population of this country.

KING: Although the Committee operates on a non-party basis in this way, it's membership is actually determined by the parties in the House of Commons, as Airey Neave explains:

NEAVE: The members of the Committee are usually chosen through the Whips, through the party organisations, and so far this system – which has been much criticised in the past – has proved very effective in this field as far as the Select Committee is concerned. And I've no reason to complain of it. We have never in fact had anyone – at least, for many years – who has raised party issues in the Committee.

KING: Are members chosen by their own party Whips on the basis of the fact that they have special interests, special qualifications, in the work of the Committee?

NEAVE: Yes. This, I think, is so. We now have more and more people who've had a scientific or engineering background or an industrial background and perhaps an educational background, and gradually we are choosing the best people for this job through the party system.

KING: The Committee got interested in the population problem about three years ago, when one of its sub-committees launched an investigation into the subject. The sub-committee devoted more than four months to reading the relevant documents and to examining no less than forty-four witnesses. Arthur Palmer was Chairman of the Committee at the time, and I asked him why this particular subject had been chosen.

PALMER: I think it was somewhat of a reaction to the concentration earlier – quite understandably, I think, and properly – of the Committee on the more mechanical subjects. But science and technology isn't strictly limited to heavy engineering or to nuclear energy or even to coastal pollution. Human matters can also be studied in a scientific fashion.

KING: One of the first things the sub-committee did was to appoint William Brass of London University as its specialist adviser. The Committee consists largely of laymen and usually calls in one or two experts in this way. How did it make use of Mr Brass's services? Arthur Palmer explains:

PALMER: He would be present with us at every session. He'd

give us a private opinion afterwards of witnesses. He would draw attention to gaps in the evidence submitted. He would assess all the written evidence, and of course he is of considerable value to the Chairman and the Clerk to the Committee in drawing up the report.

KING: The specialist adviser also helps in deciding whom the Committee should ask to appear before it as witnesses. Professor Glass tells how the invitation for him to give evidence first arrived.

GLASS: The whole thing was really quite informal. The point is that there was a consultant to the Committee, Mr William Brass, who is a very distinguished medical demographer, and he and I are colleagues in the sense that we collaborate in the two post-graduate programmes which we have. And at the same time he is a member of a committee of which I am chairman, and he knew that I was in any case writing on the prospects of population growth in this country, and I suppose he suggested to the Committee that I might be a useful witness.

KING: More generally, I asked Arthur Palmer how he and his colleagues had gone about selecting witnesses.

PALMER: There again the standard method was used, as with every other subject. We looked round for the competent authorities, those that in this case had written a great deal on this subject, or government departments that obviously had an interest in numbers of people and in social and economic questions which arise out of population density or otherwise.

KING: In addition to Mr Brass, the sub-committee had the services of one of the Deputy Principal Clerks in the House of Commons, John Sweetman. What sort of work docs he do in servicing a select committee?

SWEETMAN: All the administrative arrangements for the meetings, the general advice, giving of advice to the committee on the subjects they wish to inquire into, the topicality of them, exploratory investigation of the subjects, what they would involve in the way of work, whether they could be taken within a session. And when they have decided to embark on a particular inquiry to give them as much assistance as possible in the conduct of that inquiry.

KING: You presumably have to establish a pretty close working relationship between yourself and the chairman.

SWEETMAN: It's very important that one establishes a very close relationship with the chairman. Also very important to establish a close relationship with those members of the committee who have a particular interest in a particular subject.

KING: Just how close the relations are between the Clerk to the Committee and its senior members is attested to by the fact that, after our interview with Mr Sweetman, he waited outside to have a word with Arthur Palmer. And then and there, with tourists milling about all over the place, they decided how the Committee should go about getting a somewhat recalcitrant minister to appear before it. The sub-committee investigating population gave Professor Glass, who teaches at the London School of Economics, several weeks' notice of the day he was due to give evidence. I asked him how he went about doing his preparation.

GLASS: I don't really think I did much preparation in any formal sense. I had read the evidence, such of it as was printed and was available to me. And I had circulated to the Committee a copy of my own paper which was going to be published in any case in our journal. And I assumed, from what I knew from Mr Brass, that they were going to ask me questions largely on this paper. And, after all, I am supposed to be a demographer so that I shouldn't have been very afraid of being asked other questions on the subject.

KING: You were given in advance some indication of the general area of questioning?

GLASS: Oh yes, yes.

KING: So one afternoon Professor Glass found himself in a committee room upstairs in the House of Commons. If his day with the committee was anything like ours, and it seems to have been, the proceedings were very relaxed. A pneumatic drill somewhere in the building refused to be silenced and, despite double-glazing, at one point a witness was competing against a potted history of the House of Commons wafting in loud and clear from one of the sight-seeing boats on the river. Although the hearings are held in public and the proceedings were far from dull, the day we were there there was only one other person in the public seats. In Professor Glass's case, once he was in the room what happened next?

GLASS: I sat down. You sit rather far from the members of the Committee – at least, I did. But everyone was seated. And although it was in a formal committee room I didn't really have much sense of formality. It was not, for example, like being cross-examined, as I once was before the war, by an inter-departmental committee with an enormous horseshoe table and I was at the pole of the magnet, so to speak. And one of the members of the Committee just started – I think it was the Chairman, Mr Palmer – and people just picked up from my answers on various points with which they were particularly concerned and we went on like that.

KING: Were you impressed or not with the quality of the questions from the M.P.s?

GLASS: Yes, I think the whole thing was really very impressive. I mean these Members of Parliament are clearly not demographers, and therefore one can't expect them to be technically expert on the subject. But, leaving that aside, it seemed to me that their questions were all perfectly relevant and the kinds of questions which informed Members of Parliament should ask.

KING: Did you get anything out of the experience?

GLASS: Well, yes, I did, in a sense. I mean I found it an extremely enjoyable experience. They weren't grilling me in any way. They were obviously very friendly. They were encouraging me – at least I felt they were encouraging me – to say what I felt and what I believed as an individual, as a demographer, without any reference to what government might feel. And I felt that it was altogether very enjoyable. In fact my only regret was that I didn't have more time.

KING: Another of the expert witnesses, Sir George Godber, the Chief Medical Officer, a civil servant, appeared before the Committee together with Sir Keith Joseph, the Secretary of State for the Social Services. How much preparation did he do before giving evidence?

GODBER: I hadn't got to present the departmental evidence. I was called in with the Secretary of State, or the Secretary of State was asked to bring me, because I'm after all, a specialist officer with a certain amount of specialised knowledge in this field and I assumed they wanted to ask me about that.

KING: How much preparation did you in fact do?

GODBER: I read the briefs the Secretary of State had, I looked quickly through a lot of my own material. After all, I produce an annual report and various other reports of that nature. And I thought I'd make do with that.

KING: Population is, of course, an enormous subject. Were

you given any indication at all in advance of the kinds of questions you were likely to be asked?

GODBER: Some indication was given to the Secretary of State, and I expected to be asked collateral questions after he had answered the particular questions he'd been asked.

KING: Did either of you make a prepared statement to begin with, or did they just launch into the questions?

GODBER: The Secretary of State opened with some general comments, but not a prepared statement in the sense that one might put in prepared evidence to an inquiry in the case of a longish statement .

KING: Did you think that the M.P.s on the Committee were on the whole questioning you closely enough and asking the right sorts of questions? Did they seem to be well briefed?

GODBER: I thought they were well briefed. They caught me out on one point where they knew the figures better than I did. But if I had been on the other side of the table I daresay I could have been a bit more penetrating on some of the points. But they may not have been those that interested them.

KING: That's how it looked from the witnesses' point of view. What about from the Committee's? Members of the Committee continually emphasise that they are laymen seeking information and advice from experts. How do they cope with, say, a minister who comes along and says: 'I've decided on the best available advice that we should do this, that or the other thing'? I asked the present Chairman, Airey Neave.

NEAVE: We seek to question him very closely indeed on why he has come to this particular decision. Above all, we seek to attest whether that advice is sound. Now one of the weaknesses of the present government system of deciding the big issues of priority in research and development – for example, in computers – is that we are doubtful about the value and competence of the advice that ministers are actually receiving. And we seek to supplement that advice by calling before us in public the very best scientists. In the report we recently made on research and development, arising out of the Rothschild Report, we called some of the very best scientists in the world before us. And we have reported our recommendations to the Government. That's a function we play, besides getting at the Government's method of decision-making.

KING: The Committee can call anyone it likes to give evidence, but most of the witnesses fall into three classes. They're outside experts like Professor Glass, they're civil servants like Sir George Godber, or they're ministers like Sir Keith Joseph. Civil servants as witnesses can be a bit of a problem. On the one hand, they may have a great deal of information and knowledge that the Committee needs. On the other, they are not actually responsible for Government policy and owe their chief loyalty to their minister and their department and not to the Select Committee or Parliament. It's not surprising under the circumstances, as Arthur Palmer once said, that departmental witnesses sometimes 'show a certain caution in answering that can amount to evasion'. I put it to Mr Palmer: do members of the Committee as a result sometimes have a difficult time?

PALMER: *They* have the difficult time. *We* don't have a difficult time. They have the difficult time. We put them through their paces, of course. But they are there to protect their department and protect their ministers – that's understandable. But that's why the Committee exists, to probe and investigate.

KING: How do you in fact go about dragging information out of them?

PALMER: Well, I think that depends on the skill of the questioning in the first place. And of course the Committee does have very considerable powers. If a witness refuses point-blank to answer a question then we would write, if it was a departmental witness, to the minister objecting very strongly to the evasion or the obstinacy of his civil servant. And, if the minister then supported his civil servant, we could report the whole matter to the House. There is a difficulty under the British system, if I'm to be frank with you, and it's this: that the same majority that appoints the Committee of course controls the business of the House. There is no absolute separation of powers under the British system of government, unlike the United States system.

KING: Because civil servants sometimes do find it difficult to answer candidly, the Select Committee on Science and Technology is particularly anxious to question ministers, the men who *are* responsible. What about them when they show up? Are they forthcoming? Airey Neave claims that they can be difficult, too.

NEAVE: There are occasions when, of course, they are called

because we have progress reports on what action is being taken by the Government in answer to our recommendations. During those progress reports ministers are reluctant to answer because they have sometimes to make a statement to the House. This does raise a point: that the Select Committee, of course, is no substitute for the House as such. But it does give a much wider opportunity to ministers to spread themselves on the bigger topics than they can get – and Members also – in answering on the floor of the House. But there is, of course, a constitutional necessity that they report to the House as well as to the Select Committee. But there are certainly occasions on which they are evasive and we certainly have ways and means of seeking to break down those inhibitions.

KING: What are those ways and means?

NEAVE: Well, very close cross-examination indeed, by being very well briefed indeed on the subject, and by asking ministers to explain why it is they can't tell Parliament at the particular time.

KING: The sub-committee investigating the problem of population took its four months or so of evidence in the early months of 1970 when the Labour Government was still in power. When the Conservatives were returned, all the evidence and all the work was there; but no report had been published and indeed for a time there was some doubt about whether the main Committee would be reappointed. In the end the new Committee decided not to collect new evidence but to issue a short report based on the evidence it already had. Airey Neave talked with me about how the report was actually prepared.

NEAVE: This was rather an unusual case because a general election separated the taking of the evidence, and I took over after that general election so I hadn't been on the committee that prepared the evidence, that heard the evidence. But I was Chairman of the Committee itself and I had to study the evidence with my new colleagues – some of them had lost their seats at the election – we had quite a lot of problems in getting going again, and we looked at this evidence and worked through it and we decided that in the circumstances there was neither time nor was it desirable to go on taking more evidence – so as to establish exactly what we meant by a population policy, for instance. We found we had enough evidence to come to the conclusion that this country needed serious action by the Government in regard to population growth. And we therefore put out recommendations, really in the form of an interim report to the Government, that they should set up a special office under certain terms of reference.

KING: Who would have drafted the report that was eventually presented to the House of Commons? Is this something the Chairman would take on, or the Clerk, or who?

NEAVE: It's jointly done. In fact a good many people play a part in making up a report like that, and it's then gone over paragraph by paragraph by the Committee as a whole.

KING: How many meetings would that take?

NEAVE: It took a very great many, the population one. One must remember that even eighteen months ago this was a highly emotive subject (it's much more accepted now) and we found it took us a very long time.

KING: In its report the Committee didn't attempt to say what a population policy for Britain should be. Instead, it recommended simply that Britain should in fact have a population policy and that, as Airey Neave has said, a special office directly responsible to the Prime Minister should be set up to work out the details. But the Government wasn't prepared to go even that far. It refused to say whether or not it should have a policy, and it refused to set up the special office. Instead, it set up a small panel of experts to look further into the whole subject. Given this pretty negative reaction, I asked Airey Neave: 'What steps has the Committee been taking since to try to bring pressure on the Government?'

NEAVE: The Government reply was disappointing because they simply set up a rather part-time panel to consider population, and we have now as a result of that called evidence from two Cabinet Ministers – Mr Carr, the Lord President of the Council, and from Sir Keith Joseph, the Secretary for Social Services – to report to us on what is now happening. We now have to report to the House on that evidence. But the action we took in calling them at this stage arose from correspondence which I had with the Prime Minister, which was of considerable importance, in March, in which I said that in future I hoped that ministers would reply to our reports within six months. If not, they should come before the Committee and personally report progress. This was a considerable innovation. The Prime Minister agreed to this quite readily.

KING: The Government, in other words, may not tell the Committee what the Committee wants to hear, but at least in future it will tell it something – and not too long after the Committee has expressed its views. One of the things that gives weight to this particular Select Committee's reports is that gradually it's building up a strongly held collective opinion about the subjects it deals with, so that the Government finds itself confronted with a group of M.P.s united across party lines. In Arthur Palmer's words, the Committee . . .

PALMER: . . . begins to build up a tradition. As you say, a collective view, a collective understanding, a collective way of working. And also – most important – both with the House of Commons, with the Government of the day, and with outside scientific opinion, it builds up its own prestige, or at least I hope it does.

KING: And, having developed a collective view, it begins to function as a pressure group with respect to government.

PALMER: It should be, in any case, from the beginning a pressure group on behalf of the House against government. But what I mean to say is it establishes some kind of reputation of its own. And this makes it very difficult for ministers and for governments to treat it lightly. Nor could they easily wind it up, if it's been doing useful work.

KING: This phrase, 'doing useful work', in fact raises the central question about select committees. They exist not primarily to conduct interesting investigations, or to gain publicity for particular issues, or even to make M.P.s better informed. They exist mainly to influence Government policy. If they have no influence on policy, then they are not really doing useful work. Of the various people we talked to, Sir George Godber was perhaps the most sceptical. I asked him the same question I asked Professor Glass: had he enjoyed the experience of appearing before the Committee? Had he found it useful?

GODBER: I think it's always interesting to see the sort of things that are exercising the minds of the Members of Parliament. I could have used my time in other ways of not less interest.

KING: More to the point, has any department Sir George Godber is associated with been influenced by the Select Committee?

'Let's suppose the Committee didn't exist. Would your life be very different or different at all?'

GODBER: I don't think that it would be different. One, of course, reads their reports and that's one of the things that might influence one in further conclusions, and the Department would think very seriously about what it should do in response to recommendations. But you were really talking to me. And my side of this is to provide some parts of the expert knowledge that the Department needs in order to reach conclusions on its programme.

KING: John Sweetman, from his vantage-point as Clerk to the Committee, is persuaded that the Committee, within its terms of reference, is doing a good job.

SWEETMAN: It's early days yet still, because the first, the real, specialist committees were only appointed in 1966, so we are still feeling our way. But I think that both press comment, television comment, and the reaction of the Government to our reports, or to the Committee's reports I should say, have indicated that they are doing a job which is worth while.

KING: Within the specific field of population, how much influence does Arthur Palmer think the Committee has had?

PALMER: A little. Oh yes, a little. I mean, after all, they have at least accepted it is a problem which should be looked at, and a special departmental committee of inquiry is now at work. I don't think that would have come about if it hadn't been for the report of the Select Committee. No one should suggest that the recommendations of the Select Committee should be automatically carried out, because after all if that were the case then we would be the Government, whilst ministers are the Government. But, if they don't do what we suggest after taking evidence and after consideration on our part, then we think they should at least give us an explanation.

KING: Am I right in thinking that you are satisfied that in the community of people who make scientific and technological policy in this country the Select Committee is a part, an integral part?

PALMER: Oh yes, that's what I was referring to earlier when I talked about the prestige of the Committee with outside opinion. And by 'outside' opinion – and I don't say this in any superior way – but, when you are dealing with technical and scientific subjects, it's bound to be expert opinion.

KING: In short, the Select Committee has established itself as a body that ministers and civil servants feel they have to pay at least some attention to. This is also the view of Airey Neave, the present Chairman. 'What reason,' I asked him, 'do you have to think that the Government took your report on population at all seriously?'

NEAVE: I think they took it seriously in the sense that they discussed whether there should be a population policy and decided that they couldn't come to that conclusion, which after all was pretty much the conclusion we came to without further evidence. What may be felt to be disappointing is they've so far made such little progress with this panel in evolving that policy. We don't expect to hear much about this until the middle of next year, for example. I think 'a low profile' is the civil service term used when one is going to do things in a rather low key.

KING: But in general are you satisfied that the Committee is making some sort of impact, that the government machine is actually being affected by the fact that you exist and are doing the the kind of work you're doing?

NEAVE: I am quite sure it is. I'm quite sure that it is having a big influence. It's only been going for five years, this particular Committee, and it has made enormous strides in that time.

KING: Five or six years is indeed a short period, given the timescale that modern Governments have to work to. And it's too early to say how much influence the Select Committee on Science and Technology will have in the long run. The Committee has no power over Governments, all it can do is try to persuade them. It has the advantage over comparable groups outside the House of Commons that it can insist that civil servants and ministers appear before it; and also that, if M.P.s of all parties share a common view, the Government of the day if it disagrees must at least give reasons why it does. Perhaps the most important single thing select committees can do was contained in that remark of Arthur Palmer's a moment ago. 'The Government have at least accepted that population is a problem. I don't think,' he said, 'that that would have come about if it hadn't been for the report of the Select Committee.' And to get a Government to take a problem seriously that it hadn't taken seriously before is, after all, no mean accomplishment.

12 A Bill is Passed

Until very recently, a lot of people undoubtedly thought of the House of Commons as pretty much a rubber-stamp, at least as far as legislation was concerned. The Government introduced a Bill, it then used its majority to make sure the Bill was passed, and that was that. Parliament has been made to seem a good deal more powerful by Labour's troubles with its Industrial Relations Bill three years ago, and in 1971–72 by the present Government's narrow escapes over the Common Market. But, even so, most people are probably unaware of just what the role of the House of Commons is in the passage of a major piece of legislation, and probably tend to underestimate the impact the House can have.

During the present session there's been passing through the House of Commons a new Criminal Justice Bill. It contains some radical provisions. It makes it possible, for instance, for major criminals to be made bankrupt so that their assets can be distributed among their victims. It also makes it possible for the courts to require convicted offenders to undertake community service work in their spare time. But the Bill has attracted very little publicity – partly because it's been overshadowed by the European Communities Bill, partly because most of it isn't very controversial as between the parties.

We thought it would be interesting to have a look at what happened to this Bill in the House of Commons: to see how Parliament works when, as is true so much of the time, the two parties aren't lined up in full battledress. Sir Elwyn Jones, the Member for West Ham South, who was Attorney-General in the Labour Government, believed that some Bill on the subject was bound to be introduced at some point.

Documentary broadcast on 16 September 1972.

JONES: We thought that there would be a Criminal Justice Bill because when we were in office we set up an Advisory Council on the Penal System, two of whose committees, under Baroness Wootton and Lord Widgery, produced reports on non-custodial treatment of offenders and reparation by criminals, and it was inevitable that as a result of the work of those committees there would be a Bill.

KING: According to Mark Carlisle, the Minister of State at the Home Office, the decision to introduce a Bill in the present session was taken early in 1971. I asked him how the Bill was prepared: did civil servants start to work on it when a definite decision to introduce a Bill had been taken, or had they been working on it before?

CARLISLE: It first came up about the turn of the year; we agreed in principle that we would like a Bill. At the time we were told that time was likely to be available in the parliamentary session, and then the civil servants immediately got down to work on the details of that Bill to have it ready for the end of the year.

KING: How much work did you put in on the Bill yourself before it was actually introduced?

CARLISLE: Well, quite a lot. What happened was this, that when the first submission was put up we had a meeting with the Home Secretary and it was agreed in principle that we would like a Bill and it was agreed in principle the type of matters we'd like in it. Then it really came back to me because I took over the responsibility then under Mr Maudling, and what happened was that we then went through it and discussed the way in which we would do every part of the Bill, and then we would have a meeting on each part after that as the detailed proposals came up.

KING: One of the civil servants who worked throughout on the Bill was Michael Moriarty, an Assistant Secretary at the Home Office with a modest paper-strewn office overlooking Whitehall. How long had he been involved in the Bill before it was published?

MORIARTY: In one sense since I came to the job in April 1968, because the two Advisory Council committees on which a lot of the provisions are based were already going then, but I think in a more direct sense since about the autumn of 1970 when those two reports were published and we had a new Government and an indication from the incoming ministers that they were interested in criminal justice legislation.

KING: What part did you personally play in the preparation of the Bill?

MORIARTY: Well, I'm in charge of the small division which has general responsibility for legislation on the powers of the courts and is also the division that looks after the Advisory Council on the Penal System. So it fell to me and to my staff to report to ministers about the two reports of the Advisory Council on reparation and alternatives to imprisonment, and suggest what might be done about them. And this involved, in fact, putting a memorandum together, collecting the views of various other parts of the Office and, indeed, of other government departments that were concerned.

KING: The Bill was published in mid-November of 1971, with the second reading debate, the major debate on the principles of the Bill, taking place about a fortnight later. The opening speech that day was made by Reginald Maudling, then still the Home Secretary, and the debate was wound up by Mark Carlisle. It had already been decided that Mr Maudling would largely bow out in parliamentary terms after the second reading and that Mr Carlisle would take the committee stage and the whole of the rest of the Bill.

It's not generally realised that civil servants brief their ministers not just behind the scenes but while actual debates are going on on the floor or in committee. Michael Moriarty was present during the second reading debate and I asked him, since he's not allowed to sit next to ministers on the front bench, how he went about communicating with them.

MORIARTY: On the whole by rapidly scribbled notes, some of them things that we ourselves realise the minister is going to need from what we hear someone else saying or what we hear him saying, sometimes things that he asks us to produce. The channel of communication is the parliamentary private secretary. These are, on the whole, fairly young M.P.s, perhaps with a ministerial career before them, who – as it were – learn the trade, and I think you get to know a great deal about what the functions of government ministers are about by understudying in that sort of way.

KING: You do actually sit there, in effect, in the chamber itself? Not technically but in fact?

MORIARTY: That's right, yes. On the right of the Speaker and behind him under the Gallery there is a box, and officials sit there and listen with their papers, scribble their notes, and there's a certain amount of scope for interchange.

KING: The publication of the Criminal Justice Bill attracted the attention of one Labour M.P. who'd not previously been involved in Home Office matters. He was Edmund Dell, the Member for Birkenhead, who served at the Department of Employment and Productivity under Barbara Castle in the Labour Government. How did he come to take an interest in this particular measure?

DELL: I was thinking of being interested in this area and it so happened that my wife is a criminologist; she looked at this Bill and saw a particular section of the Bill which worried her. She didn't have any absolutely firm point of view on it but she thought that it was questionable, and she suggested to me that I discuss this aspect of the Bill in the second reading debate. It related to the repeal of a provision introduced in 1967 that certain types of sentence of imprisonment imposed on relatively minor offenders had to be suspended and the Government was proposing in the Bill to repeal this.

KING: And it was this particular point about the abolition of mandatory suspended sentences for many offenders that Edmund Dell decided to pursue.

DELL: On the second reading debate I asked the Home Office a series of questions. What had happened was that Maudling, who was the Home Secretary, had said during the opening speech on the second reading that, after the initial impact of this change, it would have the effect of reducing the prison population. It seemed to me that that was a very strange conclusion to come to and I set out during my second reading – which of course followed his – to ask questions relating to why he had come to that conclusion. The next step – and for this I do pay tribute to the Home Office, it's not a thing government departments generally do – was for the Home Office to prepare a memorandum in reply to my speech. And they sent me a copy of this memorandum and it showed, in fact, that there was no basis for what Maudling had said: that, in fact, the probable result would be to increase the prison population, not reduce it.

KING: At this stage Mr Dell made sure that he was appointed to the Standing Committee due to consider the Bill. Once a Bill's been read a second time – approved in principle that is – it's sent to a committee where amendments can be moved and the various clauses considered in much more detail. In the case of very important pieces of legislation, like the European Communities Bill, the committee may actually consist of the whole House of Commons operating under a somewhat different procedure. But most Bills, including the Criminal Justice Bill, are sent upstairs, as they say, to one of the standing committees. These committees have about two dozen members each and are, in effect, miniature Houses of Commons. The majority party in the whole House also has a majority on the committee and, as in the whole House, there are ministers and Opposition front-bench spokesmen. Standing committees are not specialised: they consider whatever Bills are sent to them and not just ones on particular topics. But, of course, if an M.P. is interested in a particular Bill, he can usually see to it that he is included on the appropriate standing committee – or at least he can try.

By the time the Committee began to consider the Criminal Justice Bill, the Labour Opposition had got itself organised for the purpose. Sir Elwyn Jones, who, it was agreed, should lead for Labour on the Bill, explains how it was done.

JONES: Well, there was a working party of those who are particularly interested, in the Home Affairs Group and the Legal and Judicial Group. And they discussed the proposed amendments and the Bill, and then we devised the sharing of the work among ourselves. There are the various stages of the Bill. At the second reading, of course, anyone could take part in the discussion, but then in the committee stage the number has to be limited and that was selected by us by agreement between those who volunteered to take part in the twenty-five sessions of the committee.

KING: Everyone agrees that the atmosphere of a standing committee is quite different from that on the floor of the House. Mark Carlisle.

CARLISLE: It's usually considerably more intimate. It's more, I think one can say, constructive. It depends a lot on the Bill. For example, on this Bill the atmosphere throughout was that people were wanting to get down and do a careful revision of the details of the Bill in a constructive manner.

KING: Michael Moriarty describes the contrast in more detail.

MORIARTY: It's a good deal easier and less formal. A committee room is I suppose not much larger than a large school classroom. The M.P.s, of whom in our case there were about twenty in all, sit at desks facing one another, so to that extent it's a sort of mini-chamber. In place of the Speaker we have a Chairman of the Committee, that's an M.P., who is on a low dais. On his left he has the House officials and the *Hansard* people. On the right of the Chairman there is Parliamentary Counsel and then the officials like myself who are there to give advice to the minister on the contents of the Bill.

KING: Let's suppose an M.P. raises a point and the minister isn't quite sure how he's going to reply: will he in standing committee, actually there and then, turn to you and mutter something to you in order to get some help?

MORIARTY: Yes, because of the geography, which it's slightly difficult to describe. We are, in fact, only a few feet away from the minister, so it's perfectly easy for a minister just to get up from his seat and take a couple of paces so that he can talk quietly to us, or he can even stage whisper from where he's sitting, or he can ask his parliamentary private secretary, sitting just behind him, to turn round and have a word with us. It is all a good deal easier; there's no need for anyone to move to and fro. And, indeed, one occasionally gets a situation where someone from the Opposition or a Government backbencher asks the minister a question and then does a bit of ad-libbing while it's perfectly clear that the minister is getting the answer.

KING: The Criminal Justice Bill contained forty-nine clauses. The Committee, as Sir Elwyn Jones said, sat twenty-five times for a total of nearly sixty-four hours. The number of speeches made was no less that 1,700, almost all of them relating to proposed amendments to the Bill. I put it to Mark Carlisle: how many of these amendment were put down for propaganda purposes of one sort or another, and how many were really intended to be constructive contributions with a view possibly to the Government's accepting them?

CARLISLE: Numerically, undoubtedly the greater number were to change detailed points from a constructive point of view. On the other hand, the major debates were probably on wider issues which had been put down really for the purpose of debating that issue.

KING: Reading amendments, one sometimes has the impression that people have put them down because they would really like to write their own, say, Criminal Justice Bill rather than have anything to do with the minister's. This is true even of Government backbenchers. Is that your impression?

CARLISLE: Oh, yes, I think that, when you have a thing as wide as the Criminal Justice Bill and you have on it people – lawyers and other people who are interested in the subject – they always try and take the opportunity of putting down new clauses to be able to debate their own real interest.

KING: The Labour Party's team on the Bill, led by Sir Elwyn Jones, were determined to concentrate fairly heavily on some parts of it.

JONES: We were particularly interested in the problems of legal aid in the magistrates' courts. We think that there are far too many people who come before the court who don't know that they have the right to legal aid if they are without means. We were particularly concerned also with the question of people being kept in custody and refused bail in far too large a proportion of cases. And we concentrated a great deal of our effort on those two points.

KING: At the same time, Edmund Dell had his interest in mandatory suspended prison sentences, and two Conservative backbenchers, Edward Gardiner and Norman Fowler, were anxious to persuade the Government to incorporate into the Bill changes in the conditions relating to jury service. In the case of the jury service amendments, Mark Carlisle found himself being pressed hard by a coalition of backbenchers on his own side and the Labour Members. Sir Elwyn Jones explains what it was all about.

JONES: At the moment, there is still an element of property qualification there, and the result of the present rules is that only a tiny proportion of juries consist of women. It has been said that juries at the present time consist largely of middle-aged and middle-class men. It's not exactly a true mirror of society.

KING: Mr Carlisle eventually did agree that the desired changes should be made. He admits candidly why he gave way.

CARLISLE: Because the Government were always in favour of legislating on the jury system but had felt at first that this was not the right context in which to do it. When we got to the committee stage I found that one was having a concerted – 'approach' I think perhaps is a better word than 'attack' – from the backbenchers on one's own side and the front bench opposite.

And there was a clear pressure to legislate at that time. We looked at it again and we made it clear that, although we couldn't do it in the Commons, the time-scale would allow us to do it while the Bill went through the House of Lords, and that we have done.

KING: The Government made at least one other important concession. The Labour Party pressed hard for the writing-in of new provisions relating to legal aid. For example, Labour wanted magistrates and judges to be required to inform defendants that they might be entitled to legal aid. The Government refused to accept Labour's amendments to the Bill, but did agree to send round a Home Office circular to the courts recommending most of what Labour was asking for. Just how this concession came about emerged in the course of my conversation with Sir Elwyn Jones, when I asked him whether, when the Bill was going through the House, he was in fairly regular private communication with the Minister.

JONES: Oh no. Well, we had occasional discussions on how matters should proceed and we had private talks about whether we could by agreement come to some compromise on some of our proposals. There were discussions of that kind.

KING: Did the discussions ever actually lead to some sort of compromise?

JONES: The Minister of State, for instance, on the question of legal aid – we were pressing that, as a matter of law, there should be written into the Bill the criteria on the basis of which legal aid should be granted. He, speaking for the Government, refused that, but gave us an undertaking that the Home Office would issue a circular to the courts. That we discussed together before the thing came back into the Committee, and that's an illustration of it.

KING: I put the same question about contacts between the two front benches in the course of the passage of the Bill to Mark Carlisle – and got another candid answer.

CARLISLE: Well, I'd like to think that throughout that Bill relations between myself personally and Sir Elwyn Jones and Mr [Sam] Silkin were extremely good. We didn't have much discussion outside the Committee on the content of the Bill, but inside the Committee I think both of us were trying to get the best Bill we possibly could.

KING: But something like the concession on legal aid – sending the circular round – is that the sort of thing you might have discussed privately?

CARLISLE: The answer to that question is yes.

KING: Given the fact that the Government did make several concessions, how far did it go into the committee stage in a frame of mind to give way on some points if a good case could be made out? Or even just for the sake of appearing conciliatory? I asked Mark Carlisle: 'At the time of the publication of the Bill, were there things in it that you already thought you might want subsequently to modify in the light of parliamentary discussion?'

CARLISLE: Well, there was a lot of experimental stuff in it, and therefore to an extent on the detail we were very open to persuasion. What I did find, and as I thought we would find – and probably this applies to all Bills of this nature – was that there really is often more argument about what's been left out than there is actually about the things that are in it.

KING: Do ministers ever put anything into a Bill with a view possibly to conceding it to the Opposition just as a ploy in the parliamentary game?

CARLISLE: Well, I don't think one ever deliberately puts something into a Bill for the purpose of abandoning it. But there's absolutely no doubt that as the Minister in charge of the Bill one is grateful to have certain concessions you can make in the context of a debate when matters are put to you.

KING: But on a number of important points the Government was *not* prepared to give way. Norman Fowler, the Conservative Member for Nottingham South, in addition to pressing for reforms in jury service, also moved an amendment relating to the life sentence for murder. He recalls what happened.

FOWLER: My amendment was that the courts should have the power – rather than to recommend a minimum period which the offender should serve – that they should have the power to fix it. And one of the aims here was to have a discussion about the life sentence, how the deterrent to murder was actually working, if indeed it was working or not. And I think that one achieved that very well. There was a debate on the floor of the House for three or four hours, a very good debate, a very sensible debate, and the amendment was only withdrawn on the assurance of the Home Secretary that he would keep an open mind until a committee of judges had reported.

KING: Nor would the Government accept Edmund Dell's amendment restoring the mandatory suspended sentence for certain classes of offenders. I asked Edmund Dell what the fate of his amendment had been.

DELL: The fate was that I was shown on all the facts and on the consequence of this decision to be absolutely right, but the Government nevertheless proposed to continue to do what they had already decided to do, despite the fact the consequences were opposite to those about which we were told by the Home Secretary on second reading.

KING: Why did Mark Carlisle not give way on the question of suspended sentences, which was pressed rather strongly?

CARLISLE: It was pressed strongly. This was a matter of principle. We had decided as a party that we opposed the mandatory provisions for suspended sentences. We'd opposed them in '67 during the Criminal Justice Bill, and we were clearly committed – and to my mind rightly committed – to abolishing them when we had the opportunity, and therefore that was perhaps the one example of where a party-political clash came on this Bill.

KING: Because the Government has a majority of its own supporters on standing committees, it can usually be confident of carrying the day if it finally decides not to give way on a particular point. All the same, the Government did find itself in some trouble over backbench Conservative efforts to use the Criminal Justice Bill as a means of reintroducing the death penalty. Sir Elwyn Jones was obviously mildly amused at the role the Labour Members played.

JONES: On the other side – and this is one of the interesting elements in the work of the Committee – we, so to speak, came to the rescue of the Government on certain matters like the death penalty. There was a move by seven of the Tory members of the Committee to restore the death penalty. We joined forces on the Labour Opposition side with the Ministers and that was defeated by, I think, ten votes to seven.

KING: And Mark Carlisle recognised this as the one moment in the history of the Bill when it looked as though it might be in jeopardy.

CARLISLE: There was one stage when an issue was being debated – namely, the abolition of capital punishment – which would in fact have really changed the whole character of the Bill and therefore the attitude probably of Members of Parliament to the Bill. And I had at that stage to point out to those of my colleagues on the Committee that, irrespective of one's own position, it might well be, if a controversial matter of that nature was added to a Bill of this kind, that the whole of the Bill might be defeated on the floor of the House.

KING: One major advantage a minister has in piloting a Bill through the House of Commons is sheer numbers: despite occasional near-embarrassments, like the one just mentioned, he can normally count on having enough votes to get his Bill carried. But he also has another major advantage: the detailed information and advice supplied by civil servants. Part of the job of civil servants working on a Bill is to take all the amendments – on jury service, suspended sentences, and so on – and brief the Minister on them, as Michael Moriaty explained:

MORIARTY: This is the main task of officials during the committee stage. Each morning the Order Paper is brought down from the Parliamentary Section as early as they can, and one then drops everything else and sets to work looking at the amendments, trying to work out exactly what an M.P. is getting at – sometimes, of course, it's quite a job – and this may be because he is approaching something in a confused way or because he's just a lot cleverer than we are on a particular matter. And then one goes through the processes of deciding how far the objective is compatible with the objectives of the Government in the Bill, and how far it's a sensible way of achieving it.

KING: How far is it part of the job of a civil servant to warn a minister of unforseen consequences of an amendment which he might perhaps be about to accept?

MORIARTY: Oh, I think that is really part of the bread-and-butter of briefing on amendments. Of course, this question, I think, raises in turn the question where the initiative lies, and I suppose this is different on different occasions. In our case, the initiative I think lay with us in the first instance. We would usually tender some briefing and advice on an amendment and, if necessary, Mr Carlisle would discuss these with us, tell us if he saw it differently, and so on. But on the whole he let us get on with working out a brief before telling us what his own thoughts were. But one can certainly see if it worked the other way round: that, if it began with the Minister saying what he thought, it would certainly be the task of the civil servant to say: 'Well, but have you considered A, B, and C?'

KING: Backbenchers and Opposition M.P.s, however, lack that sort of professional assistance. Where do they get help from? How did Edmund Dell inform himself for purposes of taking part in the Committee proceedings?

DELL: Well, here, of course, I have the great good fortune of having a wife who is very deeply acquainted with this whole area and who was therefore able to draw my attention to all the necessary material on every point on which I wanted to speak. So she was of enormous assistance.

KING: So it was then a question of simply going to the library and reading the stuff up?

DELL: It was a matter of going to the library, reading the stuff up, preparing the speech, and putting the available information before the Minister in the Committee and saying: 'This is information which has obviously not been considered in preparing this Bill.'

KING: And in addition to what an M.P. can do on his own, there are also organisations willing to help him, as well as to press their views on him. I asked Sir Elwyn Jones where he and his colleagues got their information from.

JONES: Well, you will remember that there were the reports of committees, which were the foundation of the clauses in the Bill, which we were able to call upon. But then in the background there are a large number of bodies, fortunately, in this country – this is one of our strengths as a democracy – like Justice, the British Section of the International Commission of Jurists, like the National Council for Civil Liberties, like the Howard League. There are half a dozen bodies at least who have worked on this sort of problem and whose reports and recommendations are available to us.

KING: The Criminal Justice Bill went through its committee stage in the spring of 1972. And the Bill as it emerged from committee was considered by the whole House of Commons at the report stage in May and June. It was read a third and final time in the small hours of 16 June. (One says, incidentally, 'whole House of Commons': in fact, partly because the Bill was not highly controversial, there can't have been more than about three dozen Members there at most.) And the third reading was unopposed.

Apart from what one thinks of the Bill and the various amendments, the question is: was the Bill adequately considered by the House? Was it a better Bill as it emerged from the House? Most of the people we talked to believe that it was adequately considered and did emerge improved. Sir Elwyn Jones, for example, remarked:

JONES: Generally speaking, on Bills of this kind Parliament plays a really constructive role and the duty of the Opposition ceases to be merely the duty to oppose; it has a duty to expose and to be constructive, and I think that could be well illustrated by the course of this Bill.

KING: Norman Fowler likewise thought the Bill had been very adequately considered by the House.

FOWLER: In the time I've been in the House of Commons I've been on a number of standing committees, and I thought the debate on this Standing Committee was really quite outstanding. There were some extremely good contributions from both sides. Some extremely good contributions from the Labour side, from the backbenchers on the Labour side. And I would have thought that all the major proposals were very fully discussed indeed. And it was one of the outstanding features of this Bill, where the pressure is normally upon certainly Government backbenchers to shut up, in this case they were allowed to have their say, they were allowed to make contributions, and as a result the Bill was very fully considered indeed.

KING: Only Edmund Dell dissented from this generally favourable view

DELL: No, I don't think that the system of consideration of Bills by Parliament is a satisfactory system. For example, I don't think that it is a satisfactory way of proceeding with a Bill to have a series of debates on particular issues. What one should always be able to start with is the select committee procedure, which involves Members being able to question outside experts and ministers and departmental officials about the facts.

Now, you see, you take this particular issue of the mandatory suspended sentence. One of the ways in which some of the facts about the consequence of this came out was when I was able to arrange for certain colleagues of mine on the Expenditure

Committee, which happened to be interviewing the Director-General of the Prison Service, a Home Office official, to ask him what he thought the consequence of the repeal of the mandatory provision would be, and he told them what the consequence would be. Now I was never able to put such a question to a Home Office official in the course of the Standing Committee. All I could do was put that question to the Minister and the Minister just gave me vague answers.

KING: So the present system can be criticised. And it may be that, as time goes on, Bills will begin to be referred to specialist committees which can call witnesses. What does seem to emerge, though, from our look at the Criminal Justice Bill is that, whatever else it is, the House of Commons isn't simply a rubber-stamp. The Government had to anticipate the reactions of its own supporters and the Opposition, it had to listen to their arguments, it felt it had to make concessions. The Criminal Justice Bill when it came out of the House may or may not have been a better Bill than when it went in, but it was a different Bill.

Index